At the Debt Crossroads

Protecting Yourself from Creditors

Lorena L. Saedi

ISBN:0615890652
ISBN-13: 978-0615890654

DEDICATION

To my clients, who truly are amazing people. It takes a lot of courage to realize that you have hit a wall and that you need help to overcome it. Seeing you battle to save your home, jobs, and assets has shown me what people are really made of and has made me re-evaluate the things that are truly prized assets in life: your family, health, faith, and morals.

CONTENTS

ACKNOWLEDGMENTS

Before you read my book I want to point out what this book is not. I am not here to tell you how to manage and save your money. There are experts out there much better at that than me who can provide their insights. I wrote this book because I have been doing this for a long time and I see not only the legal part of debt problems but the human part as well. We all have our reasons for getting into debt.

This book is for anyone facing debt problems. You don't need a lecture. You need options. Every choice you make has a lasting impact on your life so you need to have the best information out there to make those choices. I hope that after reading this book you will be able to decide how to approach your debt with certainty and not fear.

This book has been one of the most challenging projects of my life. Finding the time to write this book on top of managing a law firm and raising two little boys has been interesting to say the least. I would like to thank my dedicated staff for allowing me the time to focus on this project.

I would also like to thank my husband, Jaime Cisneros, who has always supported me, and my sons, Aidan and Kellan. To my mother, Dora Whisman, and my father, Essy Saedi, who have always inspired me to take chances even when most people thought I was crazy, thank you for being there to tell me that falling on your face is ok.

CHAPTER 1: LIFE CAN CHANGE IN A FLASH

"Reality Continues to Ruin My Life"- Bill Watterson

As a bankruptcy attorney I hear many stories from clients about how they thought they had everything perfectly set up and then one thing happens and it all comes falling down. Job loss, illness, divorce, and other unexpected events can throw anyone's world into chaos. For many clients it is therapeutic for them to tell me what has happened to them and how they really are responsible people. In most cases I really do believe they are correct. Their only mistake is that they did not plan for disaster. While most people are building their future they forget to look back and reassess what they have and make sure that their current way of life is protected in case of disaster.

Over the past few years, the number of American families who have found themselves in serious financial trouble has grown tremendously. Hardworking Americans who are struggling to make a good life for their family — paying their bills and working hard — lose it all when disaster strikes.

Unfortunately if you cannot pay your bills or find yourself on the loosing end of a lawsuit you could be facing the loss of everything you have worked so hard for. There are over sixteen million lawsuits filed each year in the U.S. That is more than one suit filed every two seconds.

Everyday, in courtrooms all across our nation, people just like you are losing everything they own. We hear stories about people being sued over the craziest things like hot coffee to not so crazy things like liability for your pet's actions. Lawsuits generally occur to recover one thing and that is money. All of us have assets that we could protect but don't think about it because we think we can't lose them. Your assets can easily be taken away in any lawsuit. We live in a digital age in which anyone can hire an asset investigator, who, in a few hours and for a few hundred dollars, can find out practically anything about a person's life, including, marital status, income, bank accounts, investment accounts, credit card information, real property they own, vehicles they own, unlisted telephone numbers, and much more.

Consumer Horror Stories

I recently met with a prospective client, a fellow attorney, who was facing a multi-million dollar lawsuit. The attorney was told that he was covered under the firm's malpractice insurance policy but the problem was that the firm had a $500,000 deductible! Yikes! For most of us, $500,000 is more money than we have sitting in the bank.

The issue was that this attorney had already paid off his home (which most people see as a smart move) which was worth almost a million dollars. I had to give him the bad news that he would have to sell his home and that not even bankruptcy would protect the majority of his assets. Not the outcome he expected.

This attorney shared with me that he was almost to the point that he would be leaving this firm and that he never looked at the malpractice policy due to the fact that he was "almost" out. So while he was planning his escape, life dealt him an expensive hand. For professionals, I always recommend malpractice insurance as a first line of defensive in the event that a mistake is made. We should know first and foremost how expensive litigation is and how quickly these costs can skyrocket. Even if you are a professional and do carry malpractice insurance I also advise clients to ensure that they have money saved for possibly hiring a firm to ensure that the malpractice attorneys carry on in your best interest. I know, I know. Only lawyers need to hire lawyers to make sure their lawyers are doing their job!

Perhaps the most heart wrenching situation that I see on a monthly basis are elderly clients who have depleted their retirements funds in order to pay off debts and then they are still forced to file bankruptcy. Too embarrassed to talk to their family about their financial problems they let small financial problems snowball into large ones.

I recently met with a couple in their late 60's who were facing bankruptcy. Over the course of a several years this couple had dipped into their 401K every time a financial crisis arose. When the 401K was depleted they had no choice but to finally meet with my office to consider filing bankruptcy. After reviewing their finances they were devastated to learn that bankruptcy would have been an options at the start of their financial problems and they would have never had to tap into their 401K. Now they were not only facing a retirement without their 401K but the tax consequences for the early withdrawal which would not be removed with the bankruptcy.

A few years ago the CEO of a very promising company came to see me because a competitor's lawsuit had exhausted his cash. Apparently the competition was suing this CEO on a frivolous matter in order to force him to spend money on legal fees and lose focus on the company. Unable to continue to fight the lawsuit, he was forced to not only close his company but file for Chapter 7 bankruptcy as well since he had personally guaranteed several loans. In a matter of a 12 months this CEO had gone from emerging success story to out of business.

Life changing events rarely happen when we are prepared to handle them. They usually occur when we least expect them and are the least prepared. Although you cannot plan for every event that comes up there are legal ways to protect your assets.

CHAPTER 2: HINDSIGHT IS 20/20

"Well, as we all know by now, hindsight is twenty-twenty, but it is possible to turn your hindsight into foresight."- Ellen Moore

Since my primary focus is bankruptcy law I see finances in the reverse. Viewing thousands of cases over a decade has allowed me a unique viewpoint into asset protection and human nature. As I mentioned earlier many clients need to relate to me how they built their assets and paid their bills, what they did when trouble struck, and what inevitably caused them to seek my counsel.

Financial failure isn't something that most people plan for. Going through personal bankruptcy is for many people one of the darkest times in their life. Some common preconceived ideas clients have about filing bankruptcy are:

1. They will never have access to credit again.

2. Everyone will know they filed bankruptcy.

3. Filing bankruptcy makes them a bad person.

4. They are a complete failure.

With this attitude in hand, they plowed through their retirement, threw good money after bad in worthless real estate investments, and tapped out all of their friend and family resources.

"I should have come to see you years ago" is a statement that is uttered in my offices on an almost a daily basis. Clients repeatedly tell me that have been suffering from stress, depression, and anxiety for years due to mounting financial problems and that once they had been presented the options available these problems disappeared immediately. Of course unlike some areas of the law, bankruptcy is still an issue that most people don't discuss at the lunch table at work. That leaves most people searching the internet or receiving less than accurate information from a friend of a friend.

When faced with debt issues the most common mistakes I see clients make are the following:

1. **Failing to talk to a bankruptcy protection specialist to see what their options are when problems start to arise**

No one wakes up one day and just decides to file for bankruptcy. The decision to come see me is usually made very late in the debt game and sometimes only because a garnishment or lawsuit has finally smacked my client with a large heaping dose of reality. I realize that I am the most dreaded person of the day when I first meet with clients to review their financial problems.

The way I explain options to potential clients are in terms of **Plan A, Plan B, or Plan C**. Bankruptcy is usually the last option on the table. Knowing what they can and cannot due empowers my clients to make a clear decision as to their debt and the financial path they need to take.

Remember that meeting with an attorney for a free financial analysis is an opportunity you should take advantage of. At the very worst it could be a waste of time but more often that not it can prevent you from making costly mistakes.

2. **Pulling money out of 401K and IRA's to pay back unsecured debts and arrearage on worthless real estate**

Receiving harassing phone calls and letters from creditors can push a person over the edge. Add that with the inability to make ends meet with their current incomes and it can be very tempting to withdraw from a retirement fund to pay down the debts. In fact, most all debt collectors will immediately make this "helpful" suggestion to collection targets. In almost all circumstances this is not a good way to deal with debt problems.

In the majority of cases that I see, people don't have enough retirement money to solve their debt problems. Most people who choose to use retirement funds to pay debts go through all of the allowable withdrawal funds before paying off all their debts. So not only will you lose lots of your retirement money, but you will still not be able to stop the debt collectors from calling, garnishing wages, or levying bank accounts.

Another problem with the early withdrawal of retirement funds is that this will also lead to taxes and penalties that can put you further in debt and are not dischargeable in bankruptcy. When you withdraw money from a retirement account you will have to pay early withdrawal tax penalties. Taxes are much more difficult and usually impossible to discharge in bankruptcy.

Retirement accounts are generally protected in bankruptcy. In most cases, you can keep all of the money in your retirement account when you file for bankruptcy. This means that your creditors have no right to this money. I would not advise any client to voluntarily give it to creditors when they could discharge their debts in bankruptcy and keep their retirement money. If you file bankruptcy instead of spending your retirement money, you will end up with no debts, and keep all of your retirement accounts.

3. Clinging to worthless real estate investments and transferring money from their other valuable assets

The psychological effect of losing a piece of real estate is one of the most difficult experiences for consumers to go through. On a daily basis I see clients who are horribly upside down on their home or real estate "investment" but refuse to let the property go. It may have been their first home purchase, in an exclusive neighborhood that they cannot bear to leave, or the home they grew up in. At the end of the day however, if a piece of real estate is underwater you actually own a worthless piece of property and you are for all practical purposes, renting the property.

I am never surprised when I am meeting with a new client for bankruptcy that I see multiple investment properties listed and the client tells me that these properties are the reason for their financial problems. About half of the cases I file involve clients with rental properties. In almost each case the rental property is not only underwater in property value, but it is actually drawing money away from the client in vacant tenant costs and property upkeep. To make matters worse, my clients are pulling money out of their pocket to cover the mortgage when the properties are empty or the tenants are not paying. Adding gasoline to that fire, client will then start running up credit card bills and depleting savings funds to pay for the property upkeep! This is a perfect recipe for disaster.

Depending on the foreclosure practices in your state it may be best to surrender the property back to the lender or try to short sell the property. Taking action now may prevent you from a bankruptcy filing down the road.

4. Settling with one creditor only to have another creditor refuse to settle and force them into bankruptcy anyway

I really wish I had a dollar for every client that bemoaned the fact that they should have held on to their money instead of trying to settle with an aggressive creditor just because they were afraid their credit would suffer.

For most people, filing bankruptcy is not the first thing they think of when they start to encounter financial problems. If you only have a few debts then settling with these creditors may be the best route for you. However, if you owe more than three large creditors you should carefully consider whether settlement is the best option.

Almost all of my clients have settled or made payment arrangements with one creditor only to have another creditor initiate a lawsuit and force the client to file for bankruptcy anyway. The money that the client had already spent on the settlement is essential wasted as that debt would have been erased in the bankruptcy.

5. Paying a debt settlement company to settle their bills

These days it's hard to ignore the barrage of ads from debt-settlement companies promising to cut deals on your behalf for only a fraction of what you owe. These companies seek to negotiate with your creditors to lower the overall amount owed to them. However, most people do not realize that even legitimate debt settlements will usually result in a negative mark on your credit report. In addition, if you do settle a debt you will also receive a 1099 for forgiveness of debt and face additional tax liability on the amount of debt you did not have to repay.

Unfortunately there are many unsavory companies that will promise to settle your debt but in the end leave you owing more than when you first signed up. These companies usually ask clients to stop paying on their debts and instead begin paying a set amount to the debt settlement company. The promise is that you will build up a set amount of money to settle these accounts but in reality this will usually result in your money being lost to the debt settlement company and your debts still being owed. Be wary of any company that requests an upfront fee, which is illegal in most states and should be a big red flag to run.

6. Transferring property to a family member or friend in hopes of shielding it from creditor actions

Transferring assets in order to evade creditors is a really bad idea for a few reasons. First, it usually does not work well. These transfers are fairly obvious to spot on the record and can be unwound by creditors under various circumstances both in and out of bankruptcy. Do you really think you were the first person to come up with the idea to sell your property to your brother for $100.00? Any half decent creditor attorney can unwind this transfer with a few court filings. These transfers may generally be considered a fraudulent conveyance, which, by definition, is a transfer of property made for the purpose of evading creditors, depending on the state you live in.

In bankruptcy, all transfers of property within 2 years of filing a bankruptcy petition must be reported on your bankruptcy petition. Trustee's in some states also have the ability to use the state statute to undo transfers if those statutes are longer than 2 years. If the transfer looks like it has been done in order to evade the liquidating power of a Chapter 7 bankruptcy trustee, a criminal charge of bankruptcy fraud can be raised, not to mention the possibility of having the transfer declared fraudulent in a court action by the trustee and the property liquidated anyway, or the possibility of having the bankruptcy petition dismissed.

In the end, transferring property to someone is a good way to get them sued for the recovery of the property or its basic value. Once you have started to have financial problems any transfers you make will be harshly scrutinized. As I mentioned earlier, meet with a bankruptcy attorney now to see what transaction would or would not be protected in your state. For most people, virtually all property can be protected in a bankruptcy.

7. Stop trying to keep up with the Joneses

I could write an entire book on this topic so I will keep it brief. Yes I realize that we all like to feel successful. Nothing helps you feel successful like having the same stuff as your neighbors. Having the same gadgets, vacation spots, and cars lets you feel like you fit in with your well to do neighbors. Unfortunately, that false lifestyle can also lead to insurmountable debt.

I would say about 90% of my clients have suffered from this disorder at least one time or another. Keeping up with the proverbial Joneses almost always has negative financial consequences. I hate to be the one to break it to you but the Joneses have probably maxed out their credit cards and are in debt up to their ears. The interest rate that they are paying on the mansion could pay their kid's tuition for a year! Just because you can obtain credit does not mean you should.

The idea of "keeping up with the Joneses" becomes important only when you're focusing on what others have and trying to keep score. It's easier to resist the urge to be like your neighbors when you are focused on improving your own situation and using your financial resources in a way that brings you satisfaction.

CHAPTER 3: WHAT CREDITORS CAN REALLY DO TO YOU

"Creditors have better memories than debtors."
-Benjamin Franklin

Assets are commonly defined as what a person owns. Some examples of assets are cash, checking and savings accounts, stocks, bonds, real estate, vehicles, business accounts receivables, jewelry, inventory, and prepaid expenses. You don't have to be Bill Gates to be concerned about your assets. In fact, for most of us, the threat is much more real in the event we find ourselves on the other end of a demand for money. The thought of having a lien placed on our home, our bank accounts frozen, and/or our hard earned paychecks garnished is not a pleasant one.

Every day more and more people are being overwhelmed by their debts as a result of income reduction, job loss, or the raising of interest rates by credit card companies. There are a lot of myths out there as to what creditors can do to people who are unable or unwilling to pay their bills anymore. There usually is not a day that goes by that I don't receive a call from some poor soul that has been terrified by an unscrupulous debt collector threatening jail if they don't pay up.

First, it is key to understand that not paying your bills is not a crime. Defaulting on your debts in of itself does not lead to jail. If it was a crime then there would be millions more Americans behind bars. So what can creditors really do to you?

If you fail to pay your debt obligations a creditor has several remedies which he or she can exercise. A creditor can:

1. **Contact you by phone or mail to collect the debt**

   Even with a good emergency fund, you may have found yourself struggling to pay the bills. Then the calls and letters start. Your creditors start harassing you about when you are going to pay up. Debt collection laws vary by state, but are mostly similar. Here's what you need to know about your rights under the Fair Debt Collection Practices Act and what creditors can't do when you owe them money.

Fair Debt Collection Practices Act

The Federal Trade Commission (FTC), the nation's consumer protection agency, enforces the Fair Debt Collection Practices Act (FDCPA), 15 U.S.C. §§ 1692-1692p, which prohibits debt collectors from using abusive, unfair, or deceptive practices to collect from you.

Under the FDCPA, a debt collector is someone who regularly collects debts owed to others. This includes collection agencies, lawyers who collect debts on a regular basis, and companies that buy delinquent debts and then try to collect them.

The Fair Debt Collection Practices Act regulates against creditor harassment by phone but does not explicitly say how many calls per day constitutes harassment. These calls are effectively sales calls, calls made to get you to send in money. You have the right to not accept these sales calls and it is not a crime to screen your calls. Any information they get from you helps them to decide if they should pursue a lawsuit against you.

- <u>What types of debts are covered?</u>

  The Act covers personal, family, and household debts, including money you owe on a personal credit card account, an auto loan, a medical bill, and your mortgage. The FDCPA does not cover debts you incurred to run a business.

- <u>Can a debt collector contact me any time or any place?</u>

  No. A debt collector may not contact you at inconvenient times or places, such as before 8 in the morning or after 9 at night (your time zone not theirs), unless you agree to it. And collectors may not contact you at work if they're told (orally or in writing) that you're not allowed to get calls there.

- <u>How can I stop a debt collector from contacting me?</u>

  If you decide after contacting the debt

collector that you don't want the collector to contact you again, tell the collector – in writing – to stop contacting you.

- Can a debt collector contact anyone else about my debt?

  If an attorney is representing you about the debt, the debt collector must contact the attorney, rather than you. If you don't have an attorney, a collector may contact other people – but only to find out your address, your home phone number, and where you work. Collectors usually are prohibited from contacting third parties more than once. Other than to obtain this location information about you, a debt collector generally is not permitted to discuss your debt with anyone other than you, your spouse, or your attorney.

- What does the debt collector have to tell me about the debt?

  Every collector must send you a written "validation notice" telling you how much money you owe within five days after they first contact you. This notice also must include the name of the creditor to whom you owe the money, and how to proceed if you don't think you owe the money.

- Can a debt collector keep contacting me if I don't think I owe any money?

  If you send the debt collector a letter stating that you don't owe any or all of the money, or asking for verification of the debt, that collector must stop contacting you. You have to send that letter within 30 days after you receive the validation notice. But a collector can begin contacting you again if it sends you written verification of the debt, like a copy of a bill for the amount you owe.

- What practices are off limits for debt collectors?

Harassment. Debt collectors may not harass, oppress, or abuse you or any third parties they contact. For example, they may not:

- use threats of violence or harm;
- publish a list of names of people who refuse to pay their debts (but they can give this information to the credit reporting companies);
- use obscene or profane language; or
- repeatedly use the phone to annoy someone.

False statements. Debt collectors may not lie when they are trying to collect a debt. For example, they may not:

- falsely claim that they are attorneys or government representatives;
- falsely claim that you have committed a crime;
- falsely represent that they operate or work for a credit reporting company;
- misrepresent the amount you owe;

- indicate that papers they send you are legal forms if they aren't; or
- indicate that papers they send to you aren't legal forms if they are.

Debt collectors also are prohibited from saying that:

- you will be arrested if you don't pay your debt;
- they'll seize, garnish, attach, or sell your property or wages unless they are permitted by law to take the action and intend to do so; or
- legal action will be taken against you, if doing so would be illegal or if they don't intend to take the action.

Debt collectors may not:

- give false credit information about you to anyone, including a credit reporting company;
- send you anything that looks like an official document from a court or government agency if it isn't; or
- use a false company name.

- Unfair practices. Debt collectors may not engage in unfair practices when they try to collect a debt. For example, they may not:

- try to collect any interest, fee, or other charge on top of the amount you owe unless the contract that created your debt – or your state law – allows the charge;
- deposit a post-dated check early;
- take or threaten to take your property unless it can be done legally; or

contact you by postcard.

2. Report your failure to pay to the credit reporting agencies

One of the first things creditors will do when you become more than 30 days past due it to report this to the three main credit reporting bureaus. They can also sell or lease the debts to collection agencies which report the debt to your credit and again lead to a drop in credit scores.

An entry is added to you credit report and will stay for seven years. These late payments are reported to one or all of the major credit reporting agencies, Experian, Equifax, and TransUnion. These agencies are not the only credit reporting agencies in the United States; they're just the biggest. There are dozens of smaller, regional and industry-specific credit bureaus that provide clients with credit reports and other "risk-management" services.

Your payment history makes up 35% of your

credit score. Late payments can have a significant effect on your score and affect your ability to get new credit in the future. When negative information in your report is accurate, only the passage of time can assure its removal. A consumer reporting company can report most accurate negative information for 7 years and bankruptcy information for 7-10 years depending on the chapter that you filed.

3. Sue you

Few things in life are as unsettling as the receipt of a notice that you've been sued. Being sued is highly personal and guaranteed to elevate your blood pressure. Receipt of a lawsuit send most of us into panic mode.

Practically speaking, anyone can sue anybody with or without cause by simply completing a few forms and paying a small court fee. While lawyers are ethically prohibited from engaging in conduct involving dishonesty, fraud, deceit, or misrepresentation, the definition of a "frivolous lawsuit" – a lawsuit that is without merit due to a lack of supporting legal argument or factual basis – is widely interpreted; in fact, it's so broad that virtually any plaintiff can get to court.

The Lawsuit Process

You know you are being sued when you are served with a "Summons," and "Complaint." The

Summons simply says that you are being sued and contains some information about how to respond. The Complaint sets forth the facts upon which the person suing you, the "plaintiff," bases his or her claim.

In order to be properly served the court documents must have been handed to you personally, or were handed to someone in your office or at your house and then mailed to you. Whatever you do, don't ignore the lawsuit just because you believe that service was improper. The person suing you, the plaintiff might not agree that service was improper and might get a judgment against you.

You usually have thirty days from the day you were served with the Summons and Complaint to file your response to the lawsuit. Some lawsuits, such as evictions, may have a shorter time period. Don't take any chances with these deadlines! Read the Summons to ensure you know what deadlines you have to meet.

If you do nothing after you have been served with the Summons and Complaint, the plaintiff will usually get a default judgment against you. It won't matter whether the judgment is justified; if you don't defend yourself you are found guilty in the eyes of the law.

If you decide to fight the lawsuit you can

either hire an attorney to represent you or you can represent yourself. Hiring a lawyer to represent you in the defense of the lawsuit may or may not be worth it. The only way to know is to contact an attorney and see what they charge to defend similar matters. Many people often assume that if they win they will get their attorneys' fees back from the other side. Usually this is an incorrect assumption and each side no matter who wins pays for their own legal fees. The losing side will be required to pay attorneys' fees only where there is a law that requires the loser to pay attorneys' fees or where there is a contract between the parties that provides that the loser in a lawsuit between the two must pay attorneys' fees.

If the amount you are bring sued for is less than the cost to retain an attorney you may want to just represent yourself and file a response to the lawsuit called an "Answer." You can usually obtain forms for filing an Answer from the clerk's office, at any law library, at many public libraries, or at many office supply stores. You have an absolute legal right to represent yourself in a lawsuit without hiring an attorney however you will be expected to follow the same rules as the lawyers follow.

After you file your Answer comes the most difficult and expensive part of litigation, "Discovery." Discovery is the process by which the plaintiff and the defendant try to learn about each other's case. There are, generally, three areas in discovery:

- Interrogatories: These are questions that must be answered under oath.

- Document Production: Each party may insist on seeing any relevant documents in the possession of the other.

- Depositions: These are interviews of parties and witnesses. These interviews are conducted while the witness is sworn to tell the truth, and are recorded.

During this period, either party may make "Motions." Motions are requests that the Court intervene in the lawsuit in some manner, usually by ordering the other side to do something. Each time a motion is made, you or your attorney must draft written opposition and appear before the judge to argue its merits.

Once the Discovery process is complete, the Court will usually require that the parties participate in a process called Alternative Dispute Resolution ("ADR"). The parties must make attempts to settle the case before proceeding to trial. ADR usually means mediation which is where a neutral third party is brought in to attempt to get the parties to agree on a settlement. If the case doesn't settle, then it will have to move forward to trial. A trial can be by jury or by judge. Only if both parties waive the right to a jury trial can the trial proceed before only a judge.

The key point in all of this is that you must remember that you could go through all the time and expense to defend the case and still lose! No matter how just you feel, there is substantial risk that you might not win.

If you know you owe the debt and you are unable to come to a repayment plan with a creditor, seek the advice of a bankruptcy attorney to see what your options are if the court does not rule in your favor.

4. Garnish your pay check or bank account

Ignoring a lawsuit can result in a judgment being entered against you. Once that has been obtained the creditor can take collection to another level with garnishment.

I would say the majority of my clients do not contact my office until after they start seeing a deduction from their paycheck. Imagine their surprise when their paycheck is 25% less than what they expected. For most of us, losing 25% of our paycheck can immediately throw us into financial turmoil.

When wages are attached, or "garnished," money is deducted from your paycheck and sent to the creditor. When other assets, such as property, are attached, a lien is placed on your property for the judgment amount - or for as much of the judgment amount as can be secured -- so that when a property is sold, the money obtained from the sale would be distributed first to the creditors.

Unfortunately, many consumers ignore the court notices and bury their heads in the sand. It only becomes an emergency when the lawsuit that they have been ignoring for months is now a garnishment and they losing a big chunk of their paycheck each payday. Judgments and garnishments can often be avoided if the problem is addressed early on.

Some funds exempt from garnishment

When an employer is notified of a judgment requesting wage garnishment, only a certain percentage of wages can be withheld. Most states have laws allowing the employee some income to live on, according to Title III of Consumer Credit Protection Act. Money also protected from garnishment are deductions that are legally required to be paid by the employee, such as federal, state and local taxes, unemployment insurance, state employee retirement system payments and Social Security.

State and federal law regulate the amount of money that may be garnished from a consumer's wages or bank account.

According to the U.S. Department of Labor, Title III "also protects employees by limiting the amount of earnings that may be garnished in any workweek or pay period to the lesser of 25 percent of disposable earnings or the amount by which disposable earnings are greater than 30 times the federal minimum hourly wage prescribed by Section 6(a)(1) of the Fair Labor Standards Act of 1938. This limit applies regardless of how many garnishment orders an employer receives."

So, let's say an employee nets $600 a week. Under the 25 percent formula, the maximum garnishment amount to $150 (25 % of $600). Or, using the minimum wage formula, the maximum garnishment amount is $403.50 (30 times the minimum wage of $6.55 is $196.50, which is then subtracted from the $600 net compensation). Therefore, since the rule says to use the "lesser" amount, the maximum garnishment would be $150.

Can federal benefits be garnished?

Many federal benefits are exempt from garnishment, including:

- Social Security Benefits
- Supplemental Security Income (SSI) Benefits
- Veterans' Benefits
- Civil Service, Federal Retirement & Disability Benefits

- Service Members' Pay
- Military Annuities & Survivors' Benefits
- Student Assistance
- Railroad Retirement Benefits
- Merchant Seamen Wages
- Longshoremen's & Harbor Workers' Death & Disability Benefits
- Foreign Service Retirement & Disability Benefits
- Compensation for Injury, Death, or Detention of Employees of U.S. Contractors Outside the U.S.
- FEMA Federal Disaster Assistance

Be aware however that federal benefits may be garnished under certain circumstances, such as delinquent taxes, alimony, child support, or student loans.

Wage vs. Non-Wage Garnishment

There are two different forms of garnishment: Wage and nonwage. Nonwage garnishment is a procedure where a judgment holder attempts to garnish funds in a bank account. Wage garnishment is used when it is determined the consumer is gainfully employed and has sufficient earnings to attach. If the debtor is not gainfully employed, then the garnishment process begins when a debtor's bank receives a court judgment requesting a debtor's account be frozen. Garnishment policies vary from state to state and bank to bank, so it is important to understand your state's laws on the matter.

5. Garnish your tax refund

A very common question I seem to always get around tax refund season is can a tax refund be garnished. The answer to that question is, it depends. A private creditor cannot garnish the federal government for an income tax refund. The idea that the IRS cannot be garnished is based on the federal government's sovereign immunity stemming from Article III, Section 2 of the U.S. Constitution.

Federal and state agencies are the only entities that can offset an IRS tax refund straight from the federal government before it is paid to the individual. This is accomplished through the Treasury Offset Program administered by the U.S. Department of Treasury by virtue of 26 U.S.C. § 6402(d) and 31 U.S.C. § 3720A, and other applicable laws. These provisions within the United States Code allow federal agencies and states to offset their debts through an IRS tax refund. There is a priority system utilized with the IRS at the top, followed by state agencies overseeing child support payments then other federal agencies with outstanding debts and lastly state agency debts.

6. Place a lien on your property

An unsecured creditor cannot seize your home

without a valid lien. A lien requires the creditor to obtain a judgment against you by suing you in your local court and winning the suit. It then uses the resulting civil judgment to file a claim against your property with the land records office in your county. Once filed, the judgment lien attaches to all real estate you own in the county.

The lien creates a title restriction on your mortgage title. This title restriction prevents you from refinancing your home before you pay off the judgment. In this way, the judgment lien forces you to pay off your debt if you want to sell your home.

Judgment Lien Foreclosure

Any unpaid lien holder has the legal right to foreclose on your home. Many clients incorrectly assume that only the first lien holder has this right. Judgment lien foreclosure is uncommon due to the fact that upon seizing the home, your creditor must pay off any other liens the property carries that were recorded prior to its own lien. After doing so, the creditor must sell the home for enough money to cover not only your debt, but its foreclosure costs and the amount it paid the other lien holders. This process is not an efficient use of most judgment creditors' time and resources.

Lien Expiration

The creditor's judgment - and the lien it

created - will expire after the statute of limitations for enforcement in your state passes. While the creditor has the right to renew its judgment, it must re-file any previous liens it held against your property. If other creditors filed liens after the original judgment lien, this leaves the creditor with even more debt to pay off before it can legally seize your home - making a judgment lien foreclosure even less likely.

Releasing the Lien

You can release your creditor's judgment lien and extinguish its security interest in your home by paying off the judgment in full or returning to court and successfully contesting the judgment. If the judgment is paid or overturned, the creditor has no choice but to release its claim on your property and send you a written notice of lien release.

7. Repossess your property if the loan is a secured loan

Repossession is the course of action creditors take to reclaim property that was used as collateral for a loan. When a person has defaulted on their loan obligation, repossession is the inevitable result. With that said, there are very strict rules and regulations that apply as to what exactly a creditor can and cannot repossess if an individual happens to default on a loan.

Even though loan agreements vary from lender to lender, and laws can obviously vary from state to state, there are a few wide-ranging guidelines and procedures that creditors must follow regarding what they can and cannot repossess.

After the property or item is repossessed, it can be sold commercially in order to pay off the debt the creditor is owed. Any shortage in the money made from the sale can also be collected from the debtor even if he or she doesn't have it anymore. However, a lender cannot take possession of the good unless the borrower has defaulted on the loan.

What Types of Property Can A Creditor Repossess?

There are certain types of property or assets that any creditor is well within their legal rights to repossess when an account holder defaults on a loan or credit agreement. Based on the classification of that debt, such as when that debt is in fact 'secured' by that particular piece of property, in almost all cases the creditor is permitted to repossess that property. In addition, the creditor may not be required to go before a judge to receive a ruling in court prior to repossessing that property. The following examples are the most common types of property that can be subject to repossession by a creditor once a person defaults on their loan agreement.

The Home

In almost all cases, the home mortgage loan is secured by the property that was purchased with that loan. If the homeowner fails to make their mortgage payments, the lender can exercise their right to foreclose on the home. Although the foreclosure process differs by each state there are some general steps that are taken before a property can be sold.

Foreclosure proceedings can begin after a single missed payment, but most lenders have a grace period for late payments, usually with a fee added on. After the second missed payment, you will most likely start to receive demands for payment and threats of foreclosure. Most lenders will only accept the total amount due to bring the loan current and they may also refuse any partial payments.

Once you fall three months behind this is typically when most lenders will begin the foreclosure process. This process will be in one of two ways:

- Judicial Sale: Requires that the process go through the court system, or

- Power of Sale: Sale can be conducted entirely by

the mortgage holder.

Power of sale is typically faster than the judicial route. All states allow judicial sale, while only 29 allow power of sale. If your state allows power of sale, the loan papers will usually have a clause that says this method will be used.

How the Judicial Sale Process Works:

- The lender will file a lawsuit against you.
- You will receive a letter from the court demanding payment.
- Typically, you have 30 days to respond with payment to avoid foreclosure.
- At the end of the payment period, a judgment will be entered and the lender can request sale of the property by auction.
- The auction is carried out by the sheriff's office, usually several months after the judgment.
- Once the property is sold, you're served with an eviction notice by the sheriff's office, and you must vacate the property immediately.

How the Power of Sale Process Works:

- The lender will serve you with papers demanding payment.
- After an established waiting period, a deed of trust is drawn up that temporarily conveys the property to a trustee.

- The trustee will sell the house at public auction for the lender.
- There is usually a requirement for the lender to post a public notice of sale for the auction.

Both types of foreclosure require that any other involved parties be notified of the proceedings. For instance, if the homeowner took out another loan against the house with a third party, that lender must be contacted and its loan amount must be paid from the auction's proceeds. If the third-party lender isn't paid, it can apply the mortgage to the new property owner.

Many times, the lender will actually buy the property back and attempt to sell it through the real estate market at a later date. There can also be deficiency judgments made against the borrower if the sale of the property doesn't satisfy the amount of the loan. The entire difference between the two can be required, although some states only require that difference between the fair market value of the property and the loan amount be paid.

The Automobile

Car repossession is the most common form of repossession. Everyone knows what the repo man does. Chances are you rely on your vehicle to get you where you need to go, and when you need to go, whether it's to work, school, the grocery store, or the soccer field. However if you're late with your car payments, or in some states, if you don't have adequate auto insurance, your vehicle could be taken away from you.

When you finance or lease a vehicle, your creditor or lessor has important rights that end once you've paid off your loan or lease obligation. These rights are established by the contract you signed and the law of your state. For example, if you don't make timely payments on the vehicle, your creditor may have the right to "repossess" — -or take back your car without going to court or warning you in advance. Your creditor also may be able to sell your contract to a third party, called an assignee, who may have the same right to seize the car as the original creditor.

The Federal Trade Commission, the nation's consumer protection agency, wants you to know that your creditor's rights may be limited. Some states impose rules about how your creditor may repossess the vehicle and resell it to reduce or eliminate your debt.

Seizing the Vehicle

In many states, your creditor can seize your vehicle as soon as you default on your loan or lease. Your contract should state what constitutes a default, but failure to make a payment on time is a typical example.

However, if your creditor agrees to change your payment date, the terms of your original contract may not apply any longer. If your creditor agrees to such a change, make sure you have it in writing. Oral agreements are difficult to prove.

Once you are in default, the laws of most states permit the creditor to repossess your car at any time, without notice, and to come onto your property to do so. But when seizing the vehicle, your creditor may not commit a "breach of the peace." In some states, that means using physical force, threats of force, or even removing your car from a closed garage without your permission.

Should there be a breach of the peace in seizing your car, your creditor may be required to pay a penalty or to compensate you if any harm is done to you or your property. A breach of peace also may give you a legal defense if your creditor sues you to collect a "deficiency judgment" - that is, the difference between what you owe on the contract (plus repossession and sale expenses) and what your creditor gets from the resale of your vehicle.

Selling the Vehicle

Once your vehicle has been repossessed, your creditor may decide to either keep it as compensation for your debt or resell it in a public or private sale. In some states, your creditor must let you know what will happen to the car. For example, if the car will be sold at public auction, state law may require that the creditor tell you the time and place of the sale so that you can attend and participate in the bidding. If the vehicle will be sold privately, you may have a right to know the date of the sale.

In any of these circumstances, you may be entitled to "redeem" — or buy back — the vehicle by paying the full amount you owe (usually, that includes your past due payments and the entire remaining debt), in addition to the expenses connected with the repossession, like storage, preparation for sale, and attorney fees. Another option available is that you could try to buy back the vehicle by bidding on it at the repossession sale.

Some states have consumer protection laws that allow you to "reinstate" your loan. This means you can reclaim your car by paying the amount you are behind on your loan, together with your creditor's repossession expenses. Of course, if you reclaim your car, your future payments must be made on time, and you must meet the terms of your reinstated contract to avoid another repossession.

Any resale of a repossessed vehicle must be conducted in a "commercially reasonable manner." Your creditor doesn't have to get the highest possible price for the vehicle (or even a good price for that matter). But a resale price that is below fair market value may indicate that the sale was not commercially reasonable. "Commercially reasonable" may depend on the standard sales practices in your state. A creditor's failure to resell your car in a commercially reasonable manner may give you a claim against that creditor for damages or a defense against a deficiency judgment.

Personal Property in the Vehicle

Regardless of the method used to dispose of a repossessed car, a creditor may not keep or sell any personal property found inside. In some states, your creditor must tell you what personal items were found in your car and how you can retrieve them. Your creditor also may be required to use reasonable care to prevent anyone else from removing your property from the car. If your creditor can't account for articles left in your vehicle, you may want to speak to an attorney about your right to compensation. Of course you have to be able to prove that those items where in your car at the time the car was picked up which can often be almost impossible to do. We cannot tell you how many clients have reported that laptops, purses and other items left in the car were missing when they requested these items back from the repo company.

Paying the Deficiency

Any difference between what you owe on your contract (plus certain expenses) and what your creditor gets for reselling the vehicle is called a "deficiency." For example, if you owe $10,000 on the car and your creditor sells it for $7,500, the deficiency is $2,500 plus any other fees you owe under the contract. Those might include fees related to the repossession and early termination of your lease or early payoff of your financing. In most states, your creditor is allowed to sue you for a deficiency judgment to collect the remaining amount owed as long as it followed the proper procedures for repossession and sale. Similarly, your creditor must pay you if there are surplus funds after the sale proceeds are applied to the outstanding contract obligation and related expenses, but this situation is less common.

You may have a legal defense against a deficiency judgment if, for example, your creditor breached the peace when seizing the vehicle, failed to sell the car in a commercially reasonable manner, or waited too long before suing you. An attorney will be able to tell you whether you have grounds to contest a deficiency judgment.

Electronic Disabling Devices

Some creditors might not provide you with financing unless you agree to the installation of an electronic device that prevents your car from starting if you do not make your payments on time. Many of the car dealers here in Georgia where I practice use these devices. Depending on your contract with the lender and your state's laws, using that sort of device may be considered the same as a repossession or a breach of the peace. How your state treats the use of these devices could affect your rights. Contact your state consumer protection agency or an attorney if you have questions about the use of these devices in your state.

Talking with Your Creditor or Lessor

It's easier to try to prevent a vehicle repossession from taking place than to dispute it after the fact. Contact your creditor as soon as you realize you will be late with a payment. Many creditors work with consumers they believe will be able to pay soon, even if slightly late. You may be able to negotiate a delay in your payment or a revised schedule of payments. If you can reach an agreement to change your original contract, get it in writing to avoid questions later.

However, your creditor or lessor may refuse to accept late payments or make other changes in your contract — and may demand that you return the car. If you agree to a "voluntary repossession," you may reduce your creditor's expenses, which you would be responsible for paying. But even if you return the car voluntarily, you still are responsible for paying any deficiency on your contract, and your creditor still may enter the late payments or repossession on your credit report.

Rent-To-Own Property

Any item that an individual purchases based on a rent-to-own agreement with a retail company offering those services is subject to being repossessed if the individual fails to make their scheduled payments. Companies like Aaron Rentals and Rent A Center are two companies that usually come to mind for most people. These agreements can include furniture, electronics, appliances, home improvements such as windows and HVAC units and any other type of merchandise acquired through a rental agreement with the option of purchasing the item over a specific timeframe. In most cases, these items are in fact rented until the rent-to-own agreement has been fulfilled, and the purchase price has been fully paid. Therefore, until the item is fully paid off you are never regarded as the owner of the merchandise.

The Property Pledged As Collateral

Any form of debt is considered secured if a specific item of property or asset, referred to as collateral, is used to guarantee the complete repayment of the debt, which will invariably include interest. Many small loan companies will ask that you list all of your assets of value to pledge for the loan. If you fail to repay the debt or default on the specific terms of the loan for any other reason, most states allow the secured creditor to take possession of the property without having to first file a lawsuit in court to receive a judgment permitting them to do so.

Dealing with repossession can be both embarrassing and challenging. No one wants their neighbors seeing the repo man towing their car away or carrying out their living room furniture. The real problem however is just beginning because once the property is recovered, any balance that you still owe on the contract, minus the amount the repossessed goods where sold for, will be sent to collections. Now you not only don't have the items you purchased, but you now have a negative mark on your credit and you still owe on the debt.

Can I ever be put into jail?

Debt collectors cannot put you in jail for not

paying your bills. But that doesn't stop debt collectors from trying all sorts of underhanded tactics to get you to pay.

There are no debtor prisons and being in debt is not a crime. You cannot go to jail just because you didn't repay a bank loan or a hospital bill. Any debt collector that tells you otherwise is lying and is violating the Fair Debt Collection Practices Act, as mentioned earlier in this section.

If a debt collector threatens to put you in jail, report them to the Federal Trade Commission and your state's attorney general. You can also sue the collector in federal or state court for damages, plus up to $1,000.00 and court costs.

There are however situations in which the court can be brought in to impose jail time regarding a debt owed. These are:

- Purposely not paying your taxes
- Committing fraud
- Violating a court order, such as failing to pay court ordered child support
- Trying to hide assets to avoid paying a judgment

Once a judgment has been entered however a creditor may conduct post-judgment discovery in which the debtor is ordered by the court to provide certain information and documents to the creditor. If the debtor fails to provide this information the court can issue a warrant for the debtor for contempt of court.

I recently met with man who ignored a lawsuit and had a judgment entered against him. After the judgment was entered the creditor then served him with post-judgment discovery in order to find out what assets he had available to repay the judgment. The man ignored this court order and the judge actually issued a warrant for his arrest. When he was pulled over for a traffic ticket a few months later he was arrested and had to pay a court fine for failing to appear in court.

Creditors have several avenues available against you if you fail to pay your bills on time. Once you start to fall behind creditors may threaten certain things in an attempt to get you to pay the debt. Of course you should pay your bills as agreed but if that is not possible it is important that you understand what actions can be taken against you to recover money owed.

CHAPTER 4: IRS COLLECTION

"Be wary of strong drink. It can make you shoot at tax collectors... and miss." -Robert Heinlein

One of the most frightening types of debt collection for most people is a notice from the IRS that they owe money. When financial problems start to show themselves many times taxes are the last debt that is paid. A large percentage of my bankruptcy clients have tax debt due to the fact that they just didn't file their tax returns because they knew that they would owe the tax.

Unfortunately, sooner or later the IRS will catch up with you and it is time to pay. The unsettling aspect of all of this is the IRS is not known for their compassion and they believe that ignorance of the law is no excuse. If you do find yourself on the wrong end of and IRS collection here are a few things your need to know.

The IRS has 10 Regional Compliance Centers which process all tax returns filed. The information on each tax return filed is encoded into the IRS computer at a Compliance Center. That IRS computer system will determine if there are any errors on the return and issue notices regarding errors. The Compliance Center is also responsible for initiating notices to taxpayers to collect balances due on tax returns.

If it is determined that you owe the IRS the following process takes place :

1. A notice will be automatically issued entitled

"Request for Payment," which informs you that there is a balance due on the tax return, states the amount owed, interest and penalties due, and requests payment within 10 days. This notice is statutorily required for the creation of a valid tax lien. If the liability is for individual income taxes, and the liability is relatively small, the taxpayer will normally receive four subsequent notices before the IRS proceeds to take any administrative collection measures.

2. If the liability is not paid after the initial notice, the taxpayer will receive a second notice, "Reminder," Notice 501. The IRS will issue Notice 503, "Urgent, Immediate action is required ", five weeks after the first notice. The taxpayer will receive Notice 504, "Urgent, We intend to levy on certain assets. Please respond NOW." in the mail five weeks after issuance of Notice 503 if payment is not made after that notice.

3. Notice 504 is the nastiest of the IRS letters. If the taxpayer fails to pay after Notice 504 the matter will be referred for collection by the Automated Collection System (ACS). If ACS is unsuccessful in collecting or resolving the matter the IRS will then issue Letter 1058, "FINAL NOTICE, NOTICE OF INTENT TO LEVY AND NOTICE OF YOUR RIGHT TO A HEARING. PLEASE RESPOND IMMEDIATELY." If you appeal

the tax assessment the collection will be stopped temporarily. If you do not appeal your assessment after you receive this notice within 30 days then the IRS can levy your assets.

Notice of Levy: Seizure of Assets Can Begin

If, after receiving all of these notices from the IRS you have still not contacted the IRS in an attempt to resolve your tax liability you will almost certainly find yourself on the end of a levy on your paycheck, bank accounts, and any other assets that the IRS can find.

It still amazes me that people ignore the IRS when they receive notices and intent to levy. Do they really think the IRS is just kidding? Trying to scare them? If there is one creditor that you do not want to ignore it is the IRS. No matter how painful it is, you need to contact the IRS in regards to any liability owed to either pay the debt or work out a repayment plan.

Installment Agreements and Offer in Compromise

If you know that you owe the tax liability assessed against you by the IRS your best course of action is to contact them immediately to try to either repay or settle your tax debt. The IRS Restructuring and Reform Act of 1998 requires that the IRS grant a payment plan to taxpayers who owe less than $10,000.00. You can ask for a repayment plan schedule and based on your income the IRS will determine what your monthly payment will be until the tax is paid off.

The other way you can deal with your tax debt is to submit and Offer in Compromise (OIC). You have probably seen or heard those commercials about settling tax debt for pennies on the dollar. The program that these ads are referring to is the OIC program which allows you to offer a lower amount than you owe to the IRS and settle for a percentage of the original debt. While you may reduce the tax liability owed it is not as easy as it is made to appear to reach a settlement of pennies on the dollar. In fact, most OIC's are rejected because the applicant does not even qualify for the program in the first place.

How the Offer in Compromise Works: Applying for an IRS Tax Debt Settlement

In order to apply for an IRS tax debt settlement, you first need to file IRS Form 656 Offer in Compromise. You will also need to include any documents supporting why you are unable to pay the total amount assessed against you and why you need an IRS settlement.

In order to know if you will qualify for an OIC you need to use their formula which is actually very simple.

1. The first part of the formula is your monthly disposable income, or MDI. Your MDI is the money you have left over each month after you pay all of your bills. For example, if after paying the bills each month you have $100 dollars. The IRS takes that $100 dollars and multiplies it by 48 months (in this case $4800 dollars.)

2. The second part of the formula is any equity you may have in assets; homes, property, cars,

401Ks, etc. Let's say the only equity you have amounts to $5000 dollars. Here's what your formula would look like:

$4800 dollars + $5000 = $9,800

According to the IRS formula your OIC should be $9,800. If you owe less than $9800, an OIC would not be what you want to do to resolve your tax debt.

When completing an OIC you want to make sure that you double check every detail to ensure that you have filled out everything as complete as possible and signed the form. Do not leave any section blank. If you do make a mistake, your IRS settlement will be denied. You have to include a 20% settlement with your offer so make sure that the numbers you are working from are correct.

There are many numerous stories about settling IRS tax debt all over the internet. While it is true that some people have settled their IRS debt for very low amounts, only a small percentage of people can qualify for these low IRS settlement offers.

The most obvious benefit of settling your IRS tax debt is saving money. IRS settlements quickly take care of your tax debt and you can get back to your normal life. When you choose to pay your IRS debt in monthly payments, penalties and interest continue to accrue on the account but when you actually settle your IRS tax debt, the tax debt does not continue to grow. It is paid off in a lump sum.

How Bankruptcy and the IRS Work Together

This same law regarding debtor protection governs the IRS Insolvency Unit, which handles bankruptcy cases. For most debtors the automatic stay remains in effect during the time the bankruptcy remains open, and for a specified period thereafter in order to account for any potential appeal. The automatic stay prevents the IRS from making a demand for payment, either orally or in writing, and prevents such efforts to collect the tax as the issuance of a garnishment on income or bank accounts, the seizing of assets, or offsetting a current year refund to back taxes.

Bankruptcy cases have advantages to both the debtor and the IRS. In addition to providing immediate temporary relief by staying all creditor actions against the debtor, certain bankruptcy options provide long-term relief by allowing a debtor to extend the time for payment of a debt, as in the case of a Chapter 13 filing, and also by yielding permanent relief through outright debt discharge, as in the case of certain Chapter 7 filings.

In most cases, the IRS is considered a priority creditor because the interest in the balance has likely been secured by the filing of a Notice of Federal Tax Lien. A lien is an instrument the IRS uses to set a claim on an individual's property for payment or satisfaction of a tax debt. The lien attaches to all property or rights to property the taxpayer has or acquires, and is filed in accordance with state law to make the liability public and to protect the government's interest. Because traditional debtor / creditor remedies often lead to piecemeal dismantling of a debtor's assets, a bankruptcy filing preceded by an IRS lien allows the IRS to formally reach certain assets that may have been otherwise inaccessible.

IRS tax debts may or may not be dischargeable under a bankruptcy filing. The type and age of the tax debt are both important factors. Under a Chapter 7 filing, asset or no-asset, priority taxes are not dischargeable. To the IRS, a tax debt is considered priority if the due date of the return, plus any legal extension, is within three years of the bankruptcy petition date. This three-year rule means that most aged balances may be discharged, but any recent balances will still be collectible after the Chapter 7 has concluded. A stay of collection will be enforced, but the IRS will once again pursue any tax debt that is not satisfied through payments made from assets.

There are exceptions to this three-year rule as well. A liability for a tax return that was not filed by the taxpayer, but was assessed by the IRS under the Substitute for Return program, is not dischargeable. As a collection action, after repeated notices have gone out advising a taxpayer to file, the IRS may assess a balance, based on income information reported to the IRS by all payers. The return is assessed using simple a method; no credits, multiple exemptions, deductions or losses are given. This results is a tax debt owed, and is a tool the IRS uses to encourage a taxpayer to be compliant in the filing of a true and accurate, and timely, tax return. Balances assessed under this program are not dischargeable.

Additionally, any liability resulting from what has been determined to be a fraudulent return is not dischargeable. If a debtor willfully attempted to evade taxes, and has incurred civil penalties for doing so, will also not find relief under bankruptcy dischargability rules.

The same three-year rule applies to Chapter 13 reorganization plans as well. However, since regular payments are made under a Chapter 13 filing, a tax debt has the potential to be fully paid once the plan is over. This depends on how the trustee disburses the debtor's payments. An individual filing Chapter 13 will want to keep apprised as to how payments are being applied, and the percentage amounts that each creditor is getting.

If you have tax liability make sure that you address this problem immediately. Ignoring it will not make it go away and as time goes on and interest and penalties accrue your balance will only grow. Even for those of you who are "judgment proof" at this time and don't have any assets or income to be seized, you may down the road and the consequences can be much worse. The good news is that there are several ways to deal with the IRS and get back on track with managing your debt.

CHAPTER 5: BUSINESS PLANNING

"Every morning I get up and look through the Forbes list of the richest people in America. If I'm not there, I go to work." -Robert Orben

A large portion of my clients are entrepreneurs. As a business owner myself I understand the emotional and financial commitment you make when starting a business. With that said, there comes a point in every business life cycle that an owner has to take a step back and assess the financial health of the company.

Too many times I see personal bankruptcy filings tied with a business failure. As a business owner, you face two perils that your employees do not face. First, you run the risk of having your personal assets seized to pay off your business creditors, whether the threat comes in the form of vendors demanding payment or lawsuits arising from your business. And, conversely, you also run the risk of having your business destroyed by a personal creditor who seized upon your business to pay off your personal debt.

To fully protect both your business and personal assets, you need to implement a comprehensive asset protection plan that includes purchasing insurance, using limited liability protections from formal business formation, and actively managing your finances to avoid exposure.

Why should I worry about asset protection? I have insurance.

While insurance does provide a measure of security it cannot shield your assets from all threats. Insurance policies are limited in what risks they cover and how much they pay. Either of these limitations can spell disaster to the small business owner. More importantly, insurance can't adequately protect you from economic downturns and inability to make payments to creditors.

Insurance can't protect against economic hard times

Insurance is designed to compensate, or insulate, you from loss from an "occurrence," such as a fire or a lawsuit. Insurance is not designed to protect you in the event your business falls on shaky times and you are unable to meet your bills. If you are unable to pay a supplier, that supplier can get a judgment against you for breach of contract. If you are a sole proprietor, the creditor can levy against your personal property, as well as your business assets.

Use the Correct Business Entity

So, clearly, in order to fully protect your business and personal assets, you need more than insurance. You need to take steps to place assets beyond the reach of your creditors. One of the most important steps to take is to conduct your business in a manner that separates business assets from your personal assets.

You have a variety of options when it comes to structuring your business: sole proprietorship, partnership, C corporation S corporation and limited liability company

(LLC). From the viewpoint of protecting what you have, operating your business as a sole proprietorship is a mistake. While this form of business is the easiest to start and run, all of your assets—personal and business—are within reach of any of your creditors—personal or business. Operating as a partnership does little to protect your assets. As someone who runs the business, you are probably going to be a general partner which affords only slightly more protection than operating as a sole proprietorship.

Choosing the proper legal structure

The best way to protect your personal assets from the reach of business creditors is to operate your business as an LLC or as a corporation. While both can be effective to shield your personal assets from business creditors, the LLC has some advantages in terms of simplicity and flexibility. Of course, the best structure for your business turns on many complex and personal factors, so your best bet is to use this information as a starting point for a conversation with a business advisor, such as an attorney or accountant.

If you are operating your business as an LLC or corporation, then your liability for the business's debts is limited to the assets of the business—and only those assets. Moreover, depending upon the state of company formation (and you choose the state of formation—it does not have to be where your business is located), your creditors may be prevented from reaching your ownership interest in your LLC, where they could gain control of corporate stock.

Personal Guarantees and Commingling Accounts

While forming as an LLC or a corporation generally protects your personal assets from business creditors, it's easy to trip up and cost yourself this protection. Of course, fraud will nearly always expose you to personal liability, but purely innocent actions can have the same impact. Two common mistakes are to personally guarantee a business debt or obligation and to commingle you personal and business accounts.

Personally guaranteeing business debts

When you first start a business most creditors are unwilling to accept only the company's promise to pay the bill. Many times, the creditor will insist that the owners or operators of the business also accept liability for the debt. Landlords are especially demanding in this area. This is called a personal guaranty. In general terms, a guaranty requires that the person who is primarily responsible for the debt fails to pay. Then the guaranty kicks in and the guarantor can be required to pay. This is different from a co-maker who is always equally responsible for the payments with the borrower on the debt.

The same will occur as your company is offered credit lines and corporate credit cards. Although the account is in the business name you will be required to provide your personal credit information. If your business fails then the creditor will then be able to come after you and start reporting negative information on your credit report.

As a business entity gains in age and experience showing itself responsible to pay its bills, a creditor is less likely to require personal guaranties. However, even an established business can fall on hard times. When that happens, personal guaranties are not uncommon. When that business ultimately fails, the guarantors will be on the hook for the business debts.

I recently counseled a medical professional who personally guaranteed several cosmetic medical clinics which were doing well several years ago. Unfortunately he and his business partners had to close three of the offices and as a result the landlords pursed them for the lease balances. Each partner is now looking at almost $100,000 in liability to the personal guarantee. Since each partner also works and has a job the creditor knows that they can sue each partner with a personal guarantee and garnish their wages until the debt is paid in full.

Commingling Personal and Business Accounts

When a company creditor sues a company for any debt many times they will also sue the CEO as well even if there is no guarantee under the argument that that person has used the company for personal transactions and that the corporate protection should be disregarded all together.

Whether true or not this should be a warning to all business owners that you should anticipate being sued during the life of your company and don't be surprised if a creditor uses this approach. The only way to fight this asserting is to show that you have maintained your business and personal matters separately. Make sure that you always maintain your corporation or LLC in good standing, run it like the business that it is. You must keep a wall between your business and personal life, if you want business creditors to do so. In almost of the business suits I have personally seen the owner of the company is also personally named.

Most small business owners wear a variety of hats on a day to day basis. In the bustle of running your business you need to ensure that the company is actually producing for you and not taking from you. Raiding your 401K or savings to save your company may or may not be a good idea. Skipping your tax payments to the IRS and state taxing authorities is never a good idea. Although emergencies can occur, if you see a pattern of your company needing your personal funding to make it you may need to reconsider if this company is really worth it. After all the entire reason you go into business is to make money. With proper planning and regular reassessment you an prevent your dream from becoming your nightmare.

CHAPTER 6: STUDENT LOANS

"College gives you an edge in life, but student loans will push you over."- Unknown

Millions of Americans have fallen behind on their student loans, and millions more are barely able to make their payments each month. Many economists predict student loans may be the next bubble to burst. While a college education certainly has intangible benefits even for those with a degree in medieval British literature, if you have to bury yourself in student loan debt to do it, expanding your mind might not justify the cost.

I am asked almost every day if student loans are dischargeble in bankruptcy. Over the past few years I have definitely seen a substantial increase in the number of clients seeking relief from student loan debt. In most cases, clients can not meet the tough federal hardship standards that are necessary to discharge a student loan through bankruptcy proceedings. Instead, many of these unwary parents or guardians who co-signed the student loans face the prospect of losing their life savings, cars or homes to collection agencies for aggressive private lenders.

Understanding your options and taking a strategic approach to managing your debt can have a significant positive impact on your financial net worth.

Federal vs. Private Loans

- Private Student Loans

  Student loans which are secured through a private lending institution based on the applicant's credit. It is no different than a mortgage, car loan, or credit card. The only difference involves bankruptcy. As of October 2005, most private education loans cannot be discharged through bankruptcy.

- Federal Student Loans

  There are two sources of federal loans:

  Direct Loans: originated directly through the Department of Education via the William D. Ford Direct Loan Program. When repayment starts, payments are made directly to the Department of Education.

  Federal Family Education Loan Program (FFEL): offered through various private institutions and private guarantors, but the money is guaranteed by the U.S. Department of Education. When repayment starts, payments are made to the private institution that originated the loan, or its servicers. This means that if a borrower fails to repay a loan to a private institution, that private institution will file a claim and transfer the loan to the guarantee agency. The agency has the same powers as the U.S. Department of Education to enforce the loan. If the loan stays in default for an extended period of time, the agency can then file a claim and transfer the loan to the U.S. Department of Education. At that point, the U.S. Department of Education will attempt to collect the loan.

There are many types of federal loans, however, the three most popular are Stafford, PLUS, and Perkins.

- Stafford loans can be subsidized (the government pays the interest during deferment but not forbearance), and unsubsidized (interest accrues during deferment periods).

- PLUS loans are for parents while their child is an undergraduate or for graduate students. PLUS loans are the only loans based on creditworthiness.

- Perkins loans are funded through schools directly and upon repayment, paid back to schools directly. If these loans become delinquent then the school may hire a debt collector to attempt the past due amount. The school also has the option to transfer a default Perkins loan to the U.S. Department of Education, at which point the U.S. Department of Education will attempt to collect the loan.

Default and Repayment

Unlike the collection methods we have just covered earlier in this book, collection tactics and rule are different regarding the collection for student loans. For example, when the U.S. Department of Education is collecting a defaulted loan, it can garnish wages without ever going to court.

If a borrower fails to pay a private institution that originated a loan and then defaults on that loan, the institution will forward the loan to a private debt collection agency. If the delinquency is not resolved the private institution will transfer it to the private guarantor who works with the lending institution. The guarantor then has the option of using the available remedies or transferring the loan to the U.S. Department of Education. Debt collection agencies must still comply with the Fair Debt Collection Practices Act .

If a direct loan, a loan originated by the U.S. Department of Education, enters into default, the U.S. Department of Education has a number of remedies at its disposal granted to it by the United States Congress. The U.S. Department of Education may intercept tax refunds, offset social security income, and administer wage garnishments. The U.S. Department of Education does not need to sue a borrower in court. However there are administrative rules and procedures that the U.S. Department of Education must follow before it can take these actions.

The biggest problem for borrowers is that the U.S. Department of Education may send a loan to a private debt collector to attempt debt collection. Again, these private debt collectors must comply with the FDCPA and cannot on their own intercept taxes, offset social security income, or administer wage garnishments.

There is no statute of limitation on federal student loans. A federal student loan is collectible and enforceable until you die. It is also extremely rare to see a student loan discharged in bankruptcy. You can forget all of these websites promising to show you how to discharge student loans in bankruptcy. Currently, the way the bankruptcy law is written, it is virtually impossible that a federal student loan can be discharged in bankruptcy.

Four Most Common Mistakes When Repaying Student Loans

1. Treating all debt equally

Student loan borrowers often treat all of their student loans the same during repayment. Many borrowers set up a standard payment plan and use automatic debit, essentially putting repayment on cruise control until their debt is retired. Some borrowers may choose to pay extra, but unless specified, the additional contribution is allocated across all of their loans equally. This strategy is flawed because it does not account for the wide variability in interest rates that exist across a typical student loan portfolio.

The alternative to the above repayment is to implement a targeted repayment plan that lowers the interest cost of a borrower's debt portfolio by retiring the higher interest rate loans more quickly. This is accomplished by directing a majority of the monthly loan payment toward the higher rate debt. Federal loan repayment options such as forbearance, extended payment plans, and deferment may be applied to lower interest rate loans in order to free up additional funds to target the higher rate debt. Although this strategy is rarely practiced, it should be considered as a repayment option, as the interest savings can be substantial.

2. Overusing forbearance

Graduates who carry high levels of debt and experience tight liquidity he first few years out of school may rely on forbearance to postpone their student loan payments. Many borrowers believe forbearance is the only viable option to delay payments once their grace period ends. However, borrowers must recognize that while forbearance does suspend payments, it can be a costly option because loans continue to accrue interest. For example, a graduate with $165,000 in debt at today's rates accrues close to $1,000 a month in interest during the forbearance period, all of which will be capitalized or added to the total loan balance to be repaid.

Fortunately, other options are available. For instance, deferment also suspends payments, but the government will pay the interest on the subsidized portion of the loans. Qualifying for certain types of deferment has become more difficult but the government has added payment relief program called Income-Based Repayment (IBR) and, recently, Pay As You Earn (PAYE), to provide borrowers with lower monthly payments based on their income. IBR and PAYE also include a subsidy for up to three years for qualified borrowers.

The key is to understand that forbearance can sometimes be an effective tool; however, you should always consider less costly alternatives that reduce interest cost and still provide needed liquidity.

3. Failing to learn about new repayment options

Each year seems to bring changes to programs concerning federal student loans. Unfortunately, borrowers are often unaware of how these changes may impact their financial situation. Currently, on top of the significant confusion surrounding two established federal loan relief programs - IBR and Public Service Loan Forgiveness (PSLF).

Many borrowers have not been informed of

the eligibility requirements and benefits of these programs and therefore, some borrowers who qualify are not actively taking advantage of these programs. Understanding the details of these and other programs is important as they can provide you significant cost savings if implemented properly.

Below is a summary of the federal programs:

- **IBR:** Limits monthly loan payments to 15% of a borrower's discretionary income, and for up to three years after repayment begins, the government will pay the outstanding subsidized interest. Additionally, after 25 years of qualifying payments, any outstanding balance is forgiven.

- **PAYE:** An enhancement of the IBR program, monthly loan payments is limited to 10%. Forgiveness may also be given after 20 years of monthly payments. This program is only for Fed loans disbursed after October 1, 2011 without outstanding Fed loan balance as of October 1, 2007.

- **PSLF:** Provides tax-free loan forgiveness to federal loan borrowers who make 120 qualifying payments. Borrowers employed by non-profit organizations may qualify for this program.

4. Filing tax returns without optimizing for student loan debt

How and when a recent graduate files their taxes can have a direct impact on their student loan related savings. Since IBR and PAYE monthly payments are based on a borrower's annual gross income (AGI), it is critical to enter IBR and PAYE at the appropriate time and understand how tax returns or alternative income documentation will be used to determine the monthly IBR or PAYE payment amount and affect the subsidy.

Married borrowers must also consider the benefits of choosing "married filing jointly" versus "married filing separately" status. This decision is dependent upon several factors including each partner's income and federal educational debt levels. In addition, certain graduates below an income threshold are currently able to recognize tax deductions on student loan interest paid up to $2,500 a year for at least the first 5 years of repayment. Eligibility for this and other deductions may also be affected by the filing status of married individual.

To ensure you receive the greatest savings, you should discuss your options with a tax professional who understands how your tax filing status can impact your student loan repayment.

Because student loan debt is non-dischargeable in bankruptcy in most situations it is important to always make repayment of this debt a priority. Too many times I see client who have stuck their head in the sand in regards to student loans and now faces serious consequences such as having their paycheck garnished and their tax refund taken unexpectedly.

If you are dealing with student loan debt take the time to set up a repayment plan that will work with your budget and allow you to start making a dent in the overall debt. The sooner you get started on repaying these loans the closer you will be to financial freedom in the near future.

CHAPTER 7: BEWARE OF SCAMS

"People are living longer than ever before, a phenomenon undoubtedly made necessary by the 30-year mortgage." -Doug Larson

Unfortunately when you begin to experience money problems is seems that the sharks come out. Most of the offers that someone is debt trouble receive are really only a short term fix to a long term problem. Desperation can relieve us of our common sense. I see client after client waste thousands of dollars on debt consolidation and loan modification scams. In the end, their debt situation was no better and they still had to seek bankruptcy protection to save their assets.

Loan modification scams

Thousands of homeowners who think they're getting loan modification help are actually being manipulated into giving away hundreds and thousands of dollars. But beware: dozens more illegal companies are still in business, advertising on TV, radio and on the Internet. They'll call you on the phone. They'll contact you by mail. But take the bait, and you can kiss your money - and maybe even your home - goodbye. Every month I meet with homeowners who put their faith in the wrong company and as a result have with lost their home. Even if they wanted to sue these companies for the damages that they caused most of these shady operations are already dissolved and operating under a new name for a new scam.

The feds have exposed thousands of cases of mortgage relief fraud since the housing crisis exploded. Investigators say the companies named in the three latest cases violated virtually every provision of the Mortgage Assistance Relief Services Rule (MARS Rule), which, among other things, prohibits companies from collecting up front fees for loan modification services.

The FTC says phony mortgage relief companies take the money, but deliver little or no help, and often drive homeowners deeper in debt. Many people end up losing their home.

Next time you get a chance, go to a search engine and type in these three words: mortgage assistance scams. You'll find hundreds of warnings about loan modification rip-offs, plus all the warning signs you need to know to avoid the loan mod sharks. Always be suspicious if a stranger contacts you out of the blue offering to help. And as soon anyone starts talking about payments up front-slam down that phone. Remember, it's all about getting your money.

Unfortunately during dire times people want to believe that there is hope and that their situation is differently. The typical "lure" is that you have been "pre-approved" and qualify for a modification program. Keep in mind that these companies have not seen your income statements, tax return, or current debt load. They will tell the victim that they will contact the mortgage company and get your loan modified. You give them a few thousand dollars up front with a promise to pay them another few thousand dollars (usually in the form of a post-dated check) once the loan is modified. I cannot tell you how many people contact us on the eve of foreclosure on their homes who have been duped by these companies. Sadly, not only could they have applied for the loan modification themselves but they could have saved the several thousand much needed dollars as well. Oh yes, one more word of caution. Just because a company says they have an attorney affiliated with them is no reason to trust them. Attorney or not, no one should charge you upfront for a loan modification unless they have obtained in for you first.

Debt Consolidation Scams

If the recession has left you struggling to make your mortgage and credit card payments, you may have seen ads from companies promising to help you out. The promise of being debt-free is tempting, but some unscrupulous companies will take your money and still leave you deep in debt. How do you know which companies can truly help you?

Know the Debt Consolidation Company

First, look to see if the consolidators you're considering are legitimate. Check with your state's attorney general or the Federal Trade Commission to make sure the company is real. Then, check with the Better Business Bureau to see what kind of complaints have been filed against the company. An Internet search of the company's name might also lead you to message boards and sites where you can compare notes with other customers.

Whatever you do don't just sign up with the first company you find. These companies know that you are afraid to lose your home or your car, want to get out of debt, and don't want to go into bankruptcy. Their sales representatives will play upon these fears and use high pressure sales tactics to try and get you to sign up for their services right away without comparing other companies. Resist signing up until you have spoken with at least three other companies offering the same services.

Read the Fine Print

Once you decide on a debt consolidation company make sure that you get the details on every offer in writing. What kind of fees will they charge? Are they flat fees or a percentage of your debt? Can they charge you fees later on? A common complaint is that debt consolidators will sneak in additional fees after you've signed on with them. What kind of monthly payment can they get you? How successful have they been negotiating terms for other customers? Get all the details in writing and then compare against competing offers. You should not have to pay just to get a quote or an analysis; if a company demands that you pay up front for this you need to run as fast as you can.

In my experience I have seen only a handful of legitimate companies that actually deliver what they promise. There is nothing special that debt specialists do that you cannot do yourself if you wish. If you are thinking of reaching out to one of these companies make sure you do your homework as this is one lesson that could be both painful and costly if you get it wrong.

One of the most important parts of my job as a bankruptcy attorney is to provide options to clients that don't involve bankruptcy. On many occasions bankruptcy is not the path a prospective client needs to take. In my state of Georgia there are a few debt consolidation organizations that legitimately can assist consumers with repaying debt. Credability, which used to be Consumer Credit Counseling of Georgia, will review finances with clients at no charge and provide a repayment budget based on their existing relationships with creditors. Just make sure whatever company you choose you exercise common sense in the selection. If it sounds too good to be true it probably is.

CHAPTER 8: NEGOTIATING WITH YOUR CREDITORS

"Everything is negotiable. Whether or not the negotiation is easy is another thing"-Carrie Fisher

If you decide to negotiate directly with your creditors yourself you will need to know what sort of reductions in principal and interest are reasonable, given the amount and age of your debt.

Researching this information can be time consuming and even a bit frustrating, but it will well worth it once you get on the phone or start composing letters to negotiate with creditors. Ultimately, if you choose to go it alone and negotiate directly with the credit card companies, it pays to do your homework first. You need to figure out:

- The maximum total amount you can safely afford to pay each month for all your credit card bills.
- The total amount of principal you owe for each card (that is, NOT including all current and past interest).
- The total amount of cash you can come up with.

This last item should include all sources of cash - savings, loans from family members (and even friends) - be creative. If you are going to negotiate with creditors, they are most likely going to ask for cash up front. In any event, you are most likely to get the best settlement deal if you can make one lump-sum payment.

Be forewarned

Creditors - credit card companies and the likes - are unlikely to be willing to negotiate a settlement on a debt until it is considerably past due, as in a year or more. In fact, in all likelihood, after the initial round of phone calls and threatening letters has run its course and a year or more has passed, you might well receive settlement offers from the credit card companies.

These offers tend to grow better as time passes. For instance, the first offer might be to reduce or eliminate interest. And by the third or fourth offer (assuming you have ignored or refused the previous offers), they might be proposing to reduce your principal owed, say by 25% to even 50%.

Of course, whatever they offer, you are usually best off if you submit your own reasonable counter offer.

So if they propose eliminating all interest and late charges and fees, you could counter by proposing a payment of 75% of the principal, or whatever you can realistically afford. Remember, they can only say no. And the longer your debt has gone unpaid, the less the creditors tend to be willing to settle for, as a general rule.

So if you are already a year or so past due on your payments, you would be wise to consider this method of debt settlement.

Preparing to negotiate by yourself can be pretty intimidating and takes a good deal of research to make sure you are aware of the relevant laws and regulations in your state. Also remember that if the creditor request your paycheck stubs and tax returns they will use this information against you should the negotiations fail. If you do reach a payment agreement do not provide the creditor with permission to deduct from your bank account. You can always set up online bill pay to make your payments on time and track that they were sent out on time.

Lastly, don't just accept an oral agreement with a representative on the phone. Many credit collection companies have high turnover rate and you do not want the details of your settlement to vanish just because your representative is no longer there. Whatever agreement you make with a creditor needs to be in writing!

CHAPTER 9: BANKRUPTCY: THE END OF ONE LIFE AND THE BEGINNING OF ANOTHER

"In the middle of difficulty lies opportunity."-Albert Einstein

Bankruptcy is probably one of the most misunderstood areas of the American legal systems. It seems that every day of practice brings new urban legal legends to our attention which never ceases to amaze us. The majority of my clients come to me physically, mentally and financially exhausted. A good portion of this anxiety could have been stopped if they had come in to speak with me months or years before they got to this point. Retirement accounts have been drained, marriages destroyed and medical conditions have been exacerbated by the stress brought on by financial stress.

I am not here to tell you that bankruptcy is great and a cure all for your problems. Like everything in life it has consequences. But it is not the end of the road as many financial experts would lead you to believe. In fact if you do some homework you will find that some of these "experts" have filed for bankruptcy themselves. For most of my clients it is a new beginning. Being saddled with debt is like being a slave. You really do not have any choices. You have to slave away to pay bills. In the mean time you put aside your hopes and dreams because you are caught in the debt trap. You live to work instead or work to live. Is bankruptcy the end? Yes. It is the end of being harassed. It is the end of being sued. It is the end of stress and heartache over money issues.

Why Do Bankruptcy Laws Even Exist?

Our government recognizes that when people are in debt and unable to ever pay what they owe they won't be very productive citizens. Our economy rises or falls because of productive citizens. If citizens are barely surviving this will have a dramatic effect on the country as a whole. On a personal level, if you are drowning in debt you will never be able to pay back then you will not be able to help anyone, most importantly yourself or your family. Our bankruptcy laws were enacted to provide Americans with a fresh start and a second chance to make it.

Chapter 7 and Chapter 13 Bankruptcy

For the purposes of this book I will touch on the basics of Chapter 7 and Chapter 13 bankruptcy which are available to consumers in need of financial protection. While there are several chapters of bankruptcy these two and the ones that most individuals must choose when filing.

One of the first things that I ask my clients when meeting with them is "What do you really want?". Why? Because everyone is different and have different needs that drive them. While one client may want to just walk away from everything and start over, another client may want to restructure their debt to protect co-signing friends and family. Legally, when selecting Chapter 7 or Chapter 13 the main two items we look at in regards to qualifying are your assets and your household gross income and allowable expenses.

Chapter 7

The most common form of bankruptcy is chapter 7. Chapter 7 is a relatively short and straightforward process that allows you to wipe out most, if not all, of your debt. When most people think of bankruptcy they usually think of Chapter 7.

Chapter 7 is open to most individuals and businesses that haven't filed a previous Chapter 7 bankruptcy in the last 8 years or received a Chapter 13 bankruptcy discharge in the last 4 years. Unless you fall under one of a few exemptions (current or recent active military service, for example) you must qualify to file under chapter 7 based on your income. The primary test to determine whether or not you even qualify for a chapter 7 bankruptcy is to compare your current monthly income to the median income for your state. If you make less than the state median you'll almost always qualify for a chapter 7, but don't worry if you make more. If so, you have a second opportunity to qualify under the "means test". The means test will take into account all allowable expenses which many times will bring down your income and allow you to qualify for Chapter 7 bankruptcy.

How Chapter 7 Bankruptcy Protects You

Chapter 7 bankruptcy provides at least two positive effects. First, as soon as your case is filed you start to receive protection from your creditors under the automatic stay, which is a court order that prohibits your creditors from attempting to collect the debt. This will stop debt collection lawsuits, foreclosures, and garnishments immediately. All collection calls and letters have to stop.

Second, the bankruptcy will result in the discharge of the majority of your debts. This means that your balance will become $0.00 once your case is discharged. Some debt such as student loans, domestic support obligations (alimony/child support), and a few others can't be wiped out. Credit card, medical, and repossession debt are almost always dischargeable.

The Bankruptcy Process

Filing for bankruptcy and obtaining a discharge of your debts in a Chapter 7 bankruptcy is fairly straightforward. After meeting with an attorney to review your finances you will begin by preparing your bankruptcy petition, schedules, and other documents for filing with the court. Your attorney will be able to provide you with a list of all documents required by the court in the district which you are filing. Before your paperwork can be submitted will be required to take the first of two credit counseling courses. The course can be completed online and typically takes less than an hour. Your second course will be due after your case is filed and can also be completed online.

About 30 days after filing your case you'll have your 341 Meeting of Creditors. I think that this part of the process is the one that most of my clients dread the most as most of my clients have never been in court before. The good news is that this meeting is nothing to worry about. In the district that I practice in our 341 meetings are not held in a courtroom but in a conference room.

The atmosphere is very non-threatening. You appear at the hearing with your attorney. During this meeting the bankruptcy trustee, an attorney appointed to oversee your case and represent your creditors, will take a few minutes to question you about your situation and make sure things are being done properly. Your attorney should make sure that your prepared for the questions at your 341 meeting. Creditors may also appear at these meetings, but rarely do so. Typically the only creditor that appears at these hearings are car creditors and then that is only to confirm if you are retaining or surrendering the car. Once the hearing in concluded you are done with court appearances. Most hearings do not last more than 10-15 minutes.

Once the 341 Hearing has been concluded you then just have to wait for your discharge to be issued by the court. The discharge typically takes place about 60-90 days after your 341 meeting. Once you receive your discharge you are through with your bankruptcy. You are now ready to get on with your life and enjoy your fresh start.

What Assets Have to Be Surrendered?

A chapter 7 bankruptcy is also called a liquidation bankruptcy. What that means is that, in exchange for the discharge of your debts, you are expected to surrender certain assets to the bankruptcy court so that they can be sold to pay your creditors. While the concept of a liquidation may be intimidating, but don't let it scare you. Your bankruptcy attorney can review your state's bankruptcy exemptions to see how much property is protected in a bankruptcy. Most of my clients get to keep most, if not all of their household goods, their cars, their home, their retirement fund, and more, provided they fall within certain limits. Any experienced bankruptcy attorney can tell you what is and isn't protected. Just remember to be completely forthcoming with your attorney because if you fail to disclose certain assets and transfers you could face serious repercussions.

How Will Bankruptcy Affect My Credit?

This is the number one question that is asked by my clients. In the short term, your credit will take a hit once you file for bankruptcy. However, if you've already significantly behind on your payments you really may not have much further to drop. In fact some clients see little effect on their credit because their credit score was already so low. Ironically however, for many people chapter 7 bankruptcy is the quickest way to become creditworthy again. Because you've wiped out your debt in a chapter 7 bankruptcy, you become a much better credit risk. Your debt-to-income ratio is dramatically better, which is extremely important when you go to establish new credit. They know that the money you're earning will go to repay them instead of that card that you maxed out five years ago. Most of my clients see their credit completely rebounded in about 24 months.

Chapter 13 Bankruptcy

There are many circumstances when a Chapter 7 bankruptcy is not available or practical for a consumer. When this happens, Chapter 13 bankruptcy is usually the best way to restructure your debts.

A chapter 13 bankruptcy is also called a wage earner's plan. It enables individuals with regular income to develop a plan to repay all or part of their debts. Under Chapter 13 debtors propose a repayment plan to make installments to creditors over three to five years. During this time the law forbids creditors from starting or continuing collection efforts.

Advantages of Chapter 13

Chapter 13 bankruptcy offers individuals a number of advantages over liquidation under Chapter 7. Perhaps most significantly, Chapter 13 offers individuals an opportunity to save their homes from foreclosure. By filing under this chapter, individuals can stop foreclosure proceedings and cure delinquent mortgage payments over time. If your goal is to save your home Chapter 13 is your best path and not Chapter 7. Nevertheless, they must still make all mortgage payments that come due once the chapter 13 is filed. Another advantage of Chapter 13 is that it allows individuals to reschedule other secured debts (such as vehicles, tax debt, child support, alimony) and extend them over the life of the chapter 13 plan. I have filed many emergency Chapter 13 cases due to an impending license suspension or threatened jail time over delinquent child support payments. Chapter 13 also has a special provision that protects third parties who are liable with the debtor on consumer debts. Chapter 13 acts like a consolidation loan under which the individual makes the plan payments to a Chapter 13 trustee who then distributes payments to creditors. Individuals will have no direct contact with creditors while under Chapter 13 protection.

Who is Eligible for Chapter 13?

Any individual, even if self-employed or operating an unincorporated business, is eligible for Chapter 13 relief as long as the individual's unsecured debts are less than $360,475 and secured debts are less than $1,081,400. 11 U.S.C. § 109(e). These amounts are adjusted periodically.

How Chapter 13 Works

A Chapter 13 case begins by filing a petition with the bankruptcy court serving the area where the debtor has a domicile or residence. Unless the court orders otherwise, the debtor must also file with the court: (1) schedules of assets and liabilities; (2) a schedule of current income and expenditures; (3) a schedule of executory contracts and unexpired leases; and (4) a statement of financial affairs. Fed. R. Bankr. P. 1007(b). The debtor must also file a certificate of credit counseling, just as you do in Chapter 7; evidence of payment from employers, if any, received 60 days before filing; a statement of monthly net income and any anticipated increase in income or expenses after filing; and a record of any interest the debtor has in federal or state qualified education or tuition accounts. 11 U.S.C. § 521. The debtor must provide the Chapter 13 case trustee with a copy of the tax return or transcripts for the most recent tax year as well as tax returns filed during the case (including tax returns for prior years that had not been filed when the case began). Id. A husband and wife may file a joint petition or individual petitions. 11 U.S.C. § 302(a).

In order to complete the Official Bankruptcy Forms that make up the petition, statement of financial affairs, and schedules, the debtor must compile the following information:

- A list of all creditors and the amounts and nature of their claims;
- The source, amount, and frequency of the debtor's income;
- A list of all of the debtor's property; and
- A detailed list of the debtor's monthly living expenses, i.e., food, clothing, shelter, utilities, taxes, transportation, medicine, etc.

Married individuals must gather this information for their spouse regardless of whether they are filing a joint petition, separate individual petitions, or even if only one spouse is filing. In a situation where only one spouse files, the income and expenses of the non-filing spouse is required so that the court, the trustee and creditors can evaluate the household's financial position.

When an individual files a Chapter 13 petition, an impartial trustee is appointed to administer the case. 11 U.S.C. § 1302. In some districts, the U.S. trustee or bankruptcy administrator (2) appoints a standing trustee to serve in all chapter 13 cases. 28 U.S.C. § 586(b). The chapter 13 trustee both evaluates the case and serves as a disbursing agent, collecting payments from the debtor and making distributions to creditors. 11 U.S.C. § 1302(b).

Filing the petition under Chapter 13 "automatically stays" (stops) most collection actions against the debtor or the debtor's property. 11 U.S.C. § 362. Filing the petition does not, however, stay certain types of actions listed under 11 U.S.C. § 362(b), and the stay may be effective only for a short time in some situations. The stay arises by operation of law and requires no judicial action. As long as the stay is in effect, creditors may not initiate or continue lawsuits, wage garnishments, or even make telephone calls demanding payments. The bankruptcy clerk gives notice of the bankruptcy case to all creditors whose names and addresses are provided by the debtor.

Chapter 13 also contains a special automatic stay provision that protects co-debtors. Unless the bankruptcy court authorizes otherwise, a creditor may not seek to collect a "consumer debt" from any individual who is liable along with the debtor. 11 U.S.C. § 1301(a). Consumer debts are those incurred by an individual primarily for a personal, family, or household purpose. 11 U.S.C. § 101(8).

Individuals may use a Chapter 13 proceeding to save their home from foreclosure. The automatic stay stops the foreclosure proceeding as soon as the individual files the Chapter 13 petition. The individual may then bring the past-due payments current over a reasonable period of time. Nevertheless, the debtor may still lose the home if the mortgage company completes the foreclosure sale under state law before the debtor files the petition. 11 U.S.C. § 1322(c). The debtor may also lose the home if he or she fails to make the regular mortgage payments that come due after the Chapter 13 filing.

Usually about 30 days after the debtor files the

Chapter 13 petition, the Chapter 13 trustee will hold a meeting of creditors. During this meeting, the trustee places the debtor under oath, and both the trustee and creditors may ask questions. The debtor must attend the meeting and answer questions regarding his or her financial affairs and the proposed terms of the plan.11 U.S.C. § 343. If a husband and wife file a joint petition, they both must attend the creditors' meeting and answer questions. In order to preserve their independent judgment, bankruptcy judges are prohibited from attending the creditors' meeting. 11 U.S.C. § 341(c). The parties typically resolve problems with the plan either during or shortly after the creditors' meeting. The trustee will announce his or her objections at the hearing and then the debtor and counsel will make sure that these objections are cured before the confirmation hearing in which the court approves or denies the case. Generally, the debtor can avoid problems by making sure that the petition and plan are complete and accurate, and by consulting with the trustee prior to the meeting.

In a Chapter 13 case, to participate in distributions from the bankruptcy estate, unsecured creditors must file their claims with the court within 90 days after the first date set for the meeting of creditors. Fed. R. Bankr. P. 3002(c). A governmental unit, however, has 180 days from the date the case is filed file a proof of claim.11 U.S.C. § 502(b)(9).

After the meeting of creditors, the debtor, the Chapter 13 trustee, and those creditors who wish to attend will come to court for a hearing on the debtor's Chapter 13 repayment plan.

The Chapter 13 Plan and Confirmation Hearing

Unless the court grants an extension, the debtor must file a repayment plan with the petition or within 15 days after the petition is filed. Fed. R. Bankr. P. 3015. A plan must be submitted for court approval and must provide for payments of fixed amounts to the trustee on a regular basis, typically biweekly or monthly. The trustee then distributes the funds to creditors according to the terms of the plan, which may offer creditors less than full payment on their claims.

There are three types of claims: priority, secured, and unsecured. Priority claims are those granted special status by the bankruptcy law, such as most taxes and the costs of bankruptcy proceeding. (3) Secured claims are those for which the creditor has the right take back certain property (i.e., the collateral) if the debtor does not pay the underlying debt. In contrast to secured claims, unsecured claims are generally those for which the creditor has no special rights to collect against particular property owned by the debtor.

The plan must pay priority claims in full unless a particular priority creditor agrees to different treatment of the claim or, in the case of a domestic support obligation, unless the debtor contributes all "disposable income" – discussed below – to a five-year plan.11 U.S.C. § 1322(a).

If the debtor wants to keep the collateral securing a particular claim, the plan must provide that the holder of the secured claim receive at least the value of the collateral. If the obligation underlying the secured claim was used to buy the collateral (e.g., a car loan), and the debt was incurred within certain time frames before the bankruptcy filing, the plan must provide for full payment of the debt, not just the value of the collateral (which may be less due to depreciation). Payments to certain secured creditors (i.e., the home mortgage lender), may be made over the original loan repayment schedule (which may be longer than the plan) so long as any arrearage is made up during the plan. The debtor should consult an attorney to determine the proper treatment of secured claims in the plan.

The plan need not pay unsecured claims in full as long it provides that the debtor will pay all projected "disposable income" over an "applicable commitment period," and as long as unsecured creditors receive at least as much under the plan as they would receive if the debtor's assets were liquidated under chapter 7. 11 U.S.C. § 1325. In Chapter 13, "disposable income" is income (other than child support payments received by the debtor) less amounts reasonably necessary for the maintenance or support of the debtor or dependents and less charitable contributions up to 15% of the debtor's gross income. If the debtor operates a business, the definition of disposable income excludes those amounts which are necessary for ordinary operating expenses. 11 U.S.C. § 1325(b)(2)(A) and (B). The "applicable commitment period" depends on the debtor's current monthly income. The applicable commitment period must be three years if current monthly income is less than the state median for a family of the same size – and five years if the current monthly income is greater than a family of the same size. 11 U.S.C. § 1325(d). The plan may be less than the applicable commitment period (three or five years) only if unsecured debt is paid in full over a shorter period.

Within 30 days after filing the bankruptcy case, even if the plan has not yet been approved by the court, the debtor must start making plan payments to the trustee. 11 U.S.C. § 1326(a)(1). If any secured loan payments or lease payments come due before the debtor's plan is confirmed (typically home and automobile payments), the debtor must make adequate protection payments directly to the secured lender or lessor – deducting the amount paid from the amount that would otherwise be paid to the trustee. Id.

No later than 45 days after the meeting of creditors, the bankruptcy judge must hold a confirmation hearing and decide whether the plan is feasible and meets the standards for confirmation set forth in the Bankruptcy Code. 11 U.S.C. §§ 1324, 1325. While a variety of objections may be made, the most frequent ones are that payments offered under the plan are less than creditors would receive if the debtor's assets were liquidated or that the debtor's plan does not commit all of the debtor's projected disposable income for the three or five year applicable commitment period.

If the court confirms the plan, the Chapter 13 trustee will distribute funds received under the plan "as soon as is practicable." 11 U.S.C. § 1326(a)(2). If the court declines to confirm the plan, the debtor may file a modified plan. 11 U.S.C. § 1323. The debtor may also convert the case to a liquidation case under chapter 7. (4) 11 U.S.C. § 1307(a). If the court declines to confirm the plan or the modified plan and instead dismisses the case, the court may authorize the trustee keep some funds for costs, but the trustee must return all remaining funds to the debtor (other than funds already disbursed or due to creditors). 11 U.S.C. §

1326(a)(2).

Occasionally, a change in circumstances may compromise the debtor's ability to make plan payments. For example, a creditor may object or threaten to object to a plan, or the debtor may inadvertently have failed to list all creditors. In such instances, the plan may be modified either before or after confirmation. 11 U.S.C. §§ 1323, 1329. Modification after confirmation is not limited to an initiative by the debtor, but may be at the request of the trustee or an unsecured creditor. 11 U.S.C. § 1329(a).

Making the Plan Work

The provisions of a confirmed plan bind the debtor and each creditor. 11 U.S.C. § 1327. Once the court confirms the plan, the debtor must make the plan succeed. The debtor must make regular payments to the trustee either directly or through payroll deduction, which will require adjustment to living on a fixed budget for a prolonged period. Furthermore, while confirmation of the plan entitles the debtor to retain property as long as payments are made, the debtor may not incur new debt without consulting the trustee, because additional debt may compromise the debtor's ability to complete the plan. 11 U.S.C. §§ 1305(c), 1322(a)(1), 1327.

A debtor may make plan payments through payroll deductions. This practice increases the likelihood that payments will be made on time and that the debtor will complete the plan. In any event, if the debtor fails to make the payments due under the confirmed plan, the court may dismiss the case or convert it to a liquidation case under Chapter 7 of the Bankruptcy Code. 11 U.S.C. § 1307(c).

The court may also dismiss or convert the debtor's case if the debtor fails to pay any post-filing domestic support obligations (i.e., child support, alimony), or fails to make required tax filings during the case. 11 U.S.C. §§ 1307(c) and (e), 1308, 521.

The Chapter 13 Discharge

The bankruptcy law regarding the scope of the Chapter 13 discharge is complex and has recently undergone major changes. Therefore, debtors should consult competent legal counsel prior to filing regarding the scope of the Chapter 13 discharge.

A Chapter 13 debtor is entitled to a discharge upon completion of all payments under the chapter 13 plan so long as the debtor: (1) certifies (if applicable) that all domestic support obligations that came due prior to making such certification have been paid; (2) has not received a discharge in a prior case filed within a certain time frame (two years for prior chapter 13 cases and four years for prior Chapter 7, 11 and 12 cases); and (3) has completed an approved course in financial management (if the U.S. trustee or bankruptcy administrator for the debtor's district has determined that such courses are available to the debtor). 11 U.S.C. § 1328. The court will not enter the discharge, however, until it determines, after notice and a hearing, that there is no reason to believe there is any pending proceeding that might give rise to a limitation on the debtor's homestead exemption. 11 U.S.C. § 1328(h).

The discharge releases the debtor from all debts provided for by the plan or disallowed (under section 502), with limited exceptions. Creditors provided for in full or in part under the Chapter 13 plan may no longer initiate or continue any legal or other action against the debtor to collect the discharged obligations.

As a general rule, the discharge releases the debtor from all debts provided for by the plan or disallowed, with the exception of certain debts referenced in 11 U.S.C. § 1328. Debts not discharged in Chapter 13 include certain long term obligations (such as a home mortgage), debts for alimony or child support, certain taxes, debts for most government funded or guaranteed educational loans or benefit overpayments, debts arising from death or personal injury caused by driving while intoxicated or under the influence of drugs, and debts for restitution or a criminal fine included in a sentence on the debtor's conviction of a crime. To the extent that they are not fully paid under the Chapter 13 plan, the debtor will still be responsible for these debts after the bankruptcy case has concluded. Debts for money or property obtained by false pretenses, debts for fraud or defalcation while acting in a fiduciary capacity, and debts for restitution or damages awarded in a civil case for willful or malicious actions by the debtor that cause personal injury or death to a person will be discharged unless a creditor timely files and prevails in an action to have such debts declared nondischargeable. 11 U.S.C. §§ 1328, 523(c); Fed. R. Bankr. P. 4007(c).

The discharge in a Chapter 13 case is somewhat broader than in a Chapter 7 case. Debts dischargeable in a Chapter 13, but not in Chapter 7, include debts for willful and malicious injury to property (as opposed to a person), debts incurred to pay nondischargeable tax obligations, and debts arising from property settlements in divorce or separation proceedings. 11 U.S.C. § 1328(a).

Addressing Common Bankruptcy Misconceptions

Earlier in this book I mentioned the preconceived ideas most of my clients have about bankruptcy. After over a decade of practicing bankruptcy law I can tell you that all of these assumptions are wrong.

1. You will never have access to credit again

For most of my clients, almost immediately after receiving their discharge notice from the court they are again flooded with credit offers. Cars can be obtained the day after exiting bankruptcy. I would not advise any client to just jump back into debt after receiving their financial fresh start but if they want to credit is readily available.

2. Everyone will know you filed bankruptcy

Although bankruptcy is a public record it is kept on a court database that you must have a username and password to access. Unless someone pulls your credit report they will not know that you filed for bankruptcy.

3. Filing bankruptcy makes you a bad person

This assumption always gets me because it shows how deeply programmed we are to tie our self worth into material things. Shooting an innocent person makes you a bad person. Kicking a little puppy makes you a bad person. Abandoning your kids makes you a bad person. Not paying your Chase credit card does not make you a bad person.

Many of my clients have religious issues with filing for bankruptcy protection. They believe that if they file for bankruptcy they are committing some sort of sin. There are several places in the Bible which address this issue but my favorite quote comes from Deuteronomy 15:1-2.

> "At the end of every seven years you shall grant a release. And this is the manner of the release: every creditor shall release what he has lent to his neighbor. He shall not exact it of his neighbor, his brother, because the Lord's release has been proclaimed."

I always remind my clients that I am merely getting rid of your legal responsibility to repay your debts. If down the road you rebuild your savings and want to send money to the creditors that you discharged then knock yourself out. Note: To date I have not had one client tell me that they did this.

4. You are a complete failure

Is filing bankruptcy fun? No. Is suffering from stress, depression, and anxiety fun? No. Failure is part of life. No one is immune to it. Before you resign yourself to the fact that you are a "complete failure" take a look at this of "losers" who also had to seek bankruptcy protection at one point in their lives:

- Abraham Lincoln – filed several times, due to

business failures

- Thomas Jefferson – filed several times, including after leaving office due to large debt
- Walt Disney – filed after a company owing him money filed bankruptcy
- Henry Ford – Founder of Ford Motor Company
- H.J. Heinz – Founder of the H.J. Heinz Ketchup Company
- Mark Twain (Samuel Clemens) – filed in 1894 due to failed investments
- Oscar Wilde – acclaimed poet and author
- William Fox – Founder of 20th Century Fox Film Corporation
- Dave Ramsey- Self-help guru and debt advisor

Bankruptcy is the end of one stage of your life and the beginning of another. You can either choose to take your fresh start and build again or you can keep your head down and beat yourself up which usually leads to you making the same mistakes all over again. In the end you are the only person who can make that choice.

TOP 10 MOST COMMON BANKRUPTCY QUESTIONS

Since most people are too embarrassed to ask friends and family if they have ever went through bankruptcy too many times people in financial crisis are left to the internet to deduce what will happen to them if they file for bankruptcy. I don't think I need to tell you that you cannot believe everything you read on the internet so I have compiled a list of the top 10 questions that my potential clients ask me about bankruptcy and rebuilding their financial life afterwards.

1. **I heard that they changed the law back in 2005 and now it is really hard to file for bankruptcy!**

    Yes they did change the law back in 2005. While most bankruptcy attorneys could dedicated hours of discussion on the logic in this change the fact of the matter is that is did very little to stop bankruptcy filings and in fact in some situations made it even easier! The major items that the 2005 law added to cases being are now you must show proof of your income for the last 60-90 days (depending on what chapter you file), your last filed tax return, and complete a pre-bankruptcy credit counseling course (which you can do online or over the phone and takes about 15 minutes). Not so hard and really kind of common sense stuff you would expect to do before filing for bankruptcy. Remember that there are MANY chapters of bankruptcy as well so just because you don't fit into one does not mean that you don't qualify for another form of bankruptcy protection. Most bankruptcy attorneys offer FREE consultations so I always recommend that BEFORE you are garnished or about to be evicted go talk to an experienced bankruptcy attorney to find out about your options.

2. **If I file for bankruptcy will my information be "Googleable?"**

This question never used to come up but now a days in the era of every mug shot now being broadcast on the internet I understand my client's concern. The answer however is no. Although filing for bankruptcy is a public record in order to access that information you have to have a username and password to the court's PACER website in order to search for someone's case. You cannot put someone's name into Google and see their bankruptcy information.

3. **If I file for bankruptcy will my credit be ruined for 10 years?**

This is probably the most asked question of my clients. The answer is no and here is why. Yes, if you file a Chapter 7 bankruptcy it will be listed on your credit report for 10 years from the date of filing. A Chapter 13 will be listed on your credit report for 7 years. However, the typical time in which it takes for your credit to rebound and get back to a good score so that you can purchase real estate and cars at a great interest rate is 24 months. Not so bad if you think about it. The reason is simple. Once you file for bankruptcy and receive your discharge you are clearing up your debt to income ratio (which is one of the key items in establishing your score). Although your credit score will take a ding when you file it will immediately start to rebound after you file because now the debt is gone and you can use time to rebuild. The majority of my clients have good credit within a year of receiving their discharge but I think 24 months is a realistic expectation provided that you pay your bills on time from that point forward.

4. Can I modify my home loan if I am in bankruptcy?

Yes! Most certainly yes and in some cases is it easier than before when you were in bankruptcy. Makes NO sense I know but we are talking about mortgage companies and please don't get me started on their processes and policies. What most people don't realize is that you can be in a Chapter 13 bankruptcy and do things like sell your home, modify your loan, buy a car, sell a car. The key is that we have to file a motion for the courts approval. NOT A BIG DEAL. We just have to ask. The court is merely acting as "Big Brother" in your case to ensure that you are not taken advantage of by creditors. By filing these motions creditors are required to provide all financial information to the court. Our firm files these types of motions all the time so don't let anyone tell you differently.

5. **What happens to my retirement savings if I file for bankruptcy?**

Nothing. That is right. You get to keep it. No one can force you to turn over savings in a protected retirement plan to creditors or the court for that matter. This is why I cringe when clients tell me about how they liquidated their 401K plan to pay off credit cards and other unsecured debts. If you are looking at liquidating your 401K PLEASE PLEASE PLEASE come speak to a bankruptcy attorney first who can at least show you some options to deal with the debt that does not involve throwing away your hard earned retirement.

6. **Will all of my creditors show up at my hearing to yell at me?**

First of all, all hearings conducted in bankruptcy court are conducted professionally. That means no one is allowed to yell, scream, hit, pinch or kick you while at the table. In all seriousness though the 341 Meeting of Creditors is usually a very non-eventful meeting which is not conducted in the courtroom in from of a judge but actually in a conference room in front of a trustee (which is just an attorney who conducts these meetings for extra money). I would say in 99% of my cases no creditor shows up at all and in the event they do show up it is a car creditor who just wants to ask what the condition of the car is and if my client really wants to keep it. No fireworks. No drama. I think that the hearing is what most of clients stress the most about because the average person does not feel comfortable in a court setting. The great things about having a bankruptcy attorney at your side at your hearing is that they can explain any questions your have and if on the rare chance a creditor shows up (most of the time an angry ex-spouse) your attorney can put them in their place and move the hearing along in a timely manner.

7. How long will it take me to buy a home again?

When I first started practicing bankruptcy law way back in 2002 it used to be that you could purchase a home 1 year after your discharge. Due to the current real estate mortgage fiasco it now typically take about 2 years from your discharge date in order to purchase another home. I have started to hear about some lenders loaning after 1 year again but I would say 2 years to be on the safe side in this current economic environment.

8. Which is worse your credit, foreclosure or bankruptcy?

If you are asking me this question then there is 99.9% chance that your credit is already in the toilet and you need to focus on your overall financial restricting and not what your credit report says. I would be lying if I said that this question never amazed me.

The answer to this question will actually depend on what you live it. If you live in a state that allows deficiency judgments to be executed against you on a property that was underwater then no only is your credit going to take a hit from the foreclosure (and be on your credit for 7 years) but you are also going to have a judgment against you for whatever amount you were underwater on the foreclosure sale.

If you file for bankruptcy protection yes it will be on your credit from 7-10 years depending on what chapter you file BUT once your file your creditors are prohibited from reporting additional negative information.

9. Which is worse on your credit, debt settlement or bankruptcy?

Either action will have an adverse affect on your credit. I have yet to see any creditor in a debt settlement agree to remove the negative information regarding the settlement from someone's credit report. That means that for every debt you settle you will have a negative impact on your credit score. Depending on how many of these you have it could be easier to file for bankruptcy and have your credit back in 2 years of less.

10. Will I lose my job if I file for bankruptcy?

If you're asking yourself this question, the short answer is no. 11. U.S.C. Section 525(b) is the section of federal law that makes it illegal to discriminate on the basis of whether or not a person has filed for bankruptcy protection.

Sometimes it's easy to lose sight of just how scary the bankruptcy process can be for clients because we, as attorneys, do this everyday. But when a client asks the question, 'Can I lose my job because I filed bankruptcy?', it really hits home. My clients are embarking on a process that, to them, is foreign, embarrassing and fraught with unknown perils. Losing their jobs would actually make their already dire financial situation even worse.

CHAPTER 10: MAKING YOUR EGO TAKE A BACK SEAT

"It is better to have a permanent income than to be fascinating." Oscar Wilde

I saved this section for the end of my book because I really think that this is the root of most people's financial problems that I counsel. I still see this in some of my friends and colleagues and at one time in my life I saw this same attitude in myself.

By the time most of my clients get to me they have let their financial mess snowball because of all things, their ego. They were too embarrassed to ask a friend or family member for advice, they didn't want their neighbor to know that their home was in foreclosure, their spouse would leave them if they knew about the financial problems, they have to drive a nice car to show that they are successful, etc. At the end of the day it is ego that prevents most people from seeking help.

Most of us let our egos get the best of them and instead of admitting that we overspent, cared more about what the Joneses where doing, spoiled our kids too much, made bad business decisions, we walk around with a huge weight on our shoulders because the mere thought of bankruptcy means failure.

As Americans we have been taught that you work hard, pay your bills, and when the times get tough you fight and don't admit defeat. I myself am first generation American on my father's side and I cannot tell you how many times he has drilled into my head how lucky I am to have been born is such a great country where opportunity is everywhere. The growth of our great nation was brought about by Christian values and a capitalistic society. Everyday, people struggle to get to American to have a chance at the dream many of us take for granted.

But another part of what makes out country so great is that we love the underdog and second chances. It is not that we ever lose but that we just keep getting up, again and again. This is what the American spirit is. Bankruptcy protection is in the Constitution. Why? Because our forefathers saw the need to protect individuals from creditors. They knew that without this some people would never be able to get a second change to rebuild their lives.

When clients remark that they cannot believe that they are here and that they are so embarrassed I often remind them of Abraham Lincoln who filed bankruptcy not once but several times. Imagine what would have happened to our country if Abraham Lincoln would not have gotten relief from his creditors. Instead of moving forward with his political career he would have had to focus on dealing with creditors. Imagine if he had been too proud to file for bankruptcy? While Abraham Lincoln may have been unsuccessful business person he was a remarkable President. Each of my client's second chances provided by bankruptcy opens new doors for them.

Over the last decade our country has seen many major corporations file for bankruptcy protection to get out of bad contracts and cut overpriced vendors. Most of these companies came back after bankruptcy as a leaner and more efficient company. Why is it that the CEO's of these companies are seen as success stories for guiding their company out of bankruptcy while when we hear about a person filing for bankruptcy we think this is such a horrible tragedy. The difference is ego. Pride can be deadly to relationships, career, finances, and every other aspect of your life if you let it control you. Learning to humble yourself when problems start to arise is the first step for a fresh start.

Oh and a word about the Joneses, they are broke! Stop comparing yourself and your family to others. You don't know how much debt they owe and even if they don't have any you have to learn to be grateful for what you have. A car and a house should not define you as a person. If it does, you have bigger problems than finances to deal with. Check your ego at the door and get your financial house in order. Especially if you have a family depending on you!

As I mentioned at the beginning of this book, I am not here to tell you how to manage and save your money. I will leave that to experts such as Clark Howard and Suze Orman. However the one thing I can impart is that living beneath your means and having power over your finances is one of the most liberating feelings in the world.

Several clients through the years have reached out to me years after going through bankruptcy and have shared their stories of rediscovering themselves and their families after breaking free from debt. While bankruptcy is not something that everyone facing money problems needs to pursue, dealing with your debt is the only way you will ever find the peace to live your life. After the last few years of the flash and crash of the real estate bubble I would definitely say that frugality and simple living are back in a big way.

CHAPTER 11: TIME TO TAKE ACTION!

As I mentioned at the beginning of this book, I am not here to tell you how to budget or make better financial choices. I am here to tell you what to do when your debt issues are now getting uncomfortable. As with any problem that you are facing you need to have a plan.

An Action Plan for Dealing with Debt

Step #1: Pull all three credit reports

You have to know who and how much you owe. You are entitled to one free credit report a year and can pull the free report at www.annualcreditreport.com. Make sure that you print out all three reports so that you can then compare them to ensure that all of the information is correct. If you see any information which is incorrect then you need to contact the credit reporting agency immediately. A very large percentage of credit reports have incorrect information so make sure your reports are up to date.

Step #2: Prioritize your debt:

1. Student Loans
2. Taxes
3. Mortgage Loans
4. Secured Loans (vehicles, boats, furniture)
5. Credit Cards

6. Personal Loans and Medical Bills

This is one of the most important steps in the process because it will set the tone for your repayment plan. It is in this step that you need to really decide just how important your home and/or car are to you. If making these payments each month is a stretch then you may need to make the decision to let one or both of these assets go.

Step #3: Establish a Repayment Plan

Once you have a complete list of your debts, you should figure out how you want to pay them. When it comes to the cost of debt, the best way to repay your debt is to pay off highest interest rate debts first. Rank your debts in order from highest to lowest according to interest rate. This is the order you'll repay your debts.

As an alternative, you might consider paying off your smallest debts first. If your high interest debts also have high balances, you could end up paying on a single account for months before the entire balance has been repaid. Since smaller debts are repaid quicker, many people prefer to pay them first. Choose the method that will keep you motivated to pay off your debts.

Now, at this point you may be looking at the amount of money needed to pay off your debt is more money that you have coming in. Your repayment plan just on credit card debts alone may take you 10 years. Considering that that you can recover your credit after 24 months coming out of bankruptcy you may want to schedule a meeting with a bankruptcy attorney to review your options.

Step #4: Decide What You Want to Keep

If you know that you cannot afford to repay all of the debt you currently have then you need to decide what you can keep. Since you don't have much of a choice in regards to student loans, let focus on those debts which you can decide to keep or surrender.

Your Self-Employed Status

Being self-employed can be one of the most exciting and agonizing careers in the world. While it is great to be your own boss you are also responsible for how much or how little you make. I see many clients who for whatever reason were unable to turn their business into a profitable venture. These business people took money from their personal accounts to keep the business going. Unfortunately this did not solve the business problem and instead created a personal problem.

Almost all of my business clients also owe payroll taxes. Are you using the money due for payroll for your operating expenses for your business? If so, you need to reevaluate your business because if you cannot operate your business without taking the payroll taxes you need to close up shop. Payroll taxes are non-dischargeable in bankruptcy. That means that if the business fails you will personally still owe those taxes.

Real Estate

Do a search on www.zillow.com to see what your home is currently worth. Then take a look at what you owe on your home and include all mortgages & home equity loans. Subtract what you owe on the home from that value. If you have equity in your home then congratulations! You are a small minority right now in the US. Retaining your home may be the best choice.

If you are significantly underwater on your home you then need to look at how much you are paying on all mortgages. If this amount is about the same as you would pay if you had to rent a similar property then you may have a reason to retain the home. However, if you could rent the same type of home for less you may want to think about short selling your property and starting over with a home that makes sense financially.

The real estate market is not coming back the way it was before the bubble bust so put that in your head right now. If you are underwater $50,000 in your home it many make sense to speak to a bankruptcy attorney who can tell you what options are available.

Vehicles

Many people purchase vehicles and then later determine that they may be in over their heads after making a few payments. Shiny new cares are fun to drive but if you are barely making ends meet and can't even imagine repair costs then you may want to trade your car in for a less expensive model.

Driving a paid off car is a great feeling. No worries that you may come outside one morning to get in your car and discover the repo man has taken it away. Don't allow one asset such as a large car payment to affect your ability to maintain your household budget and pay those bills such as rent and food which are a necessity.

If you do decide that bankruptcy is the route you need to take to wipe out your debts take note that obtaining a car after receiving your discharge is one of the easiest things to do.

Step #5: Put Your Plan into Action

Execution is the hardest part but it is also the most important part of this plan. Hopefully you have already dealt with what it was that brought you to your debt problems. If not, do it now.

Write your plan down and make sure that you give yourself a deadline to go through each step. Once you make your decision you need to make sure you stick by that plan and make sure that take some type of step each day towards accomplishing that step.

One effect I have seen this have on my clients is that once they start to establish their plan, be it filing for bankruptcy or setting up a repayment plan with creditors, they also start to correct budgeting problems which many times had brought them into debt in the first place.

Lastly, talk to a bankruptcy attorney to find out what options are available. A good bankruptcy attorney will not pressure you into filing. They will however let you know how much debt they can remove from your life. This information can help you proceed with your action plan.

About the Author

Lorena Saedi is the founder of Saedi Law Group, LLC, a consumer bankruptcy law firm based in Atlanta, Georgia with 10 offices located in Georgia.

Lorena has tried numerous matters before the bankruptcy courts in the Northern District of Georgia involving creditor actions to enforce foreclosure sales, debtor's objections to creditor claims, motions for sanctions regarding creditor abuse, and various other matters.

Lorena is a member of the State Bar of Georgia, Metro Atlanta Consumer Bankruptcy Attorney Group, National Association of Consumer Bankruptcy Attorneys, and the Atlanta Better Business Bureau.

Ms. Saedi received her B.A. in Political Science from the University of Tennessee and her J.D. from Emory School of Law. She resides in Atlanta and is married to Jaime Cisneros and has two sons, Aidan and Kellan.

www.ingramcontent.com/pod-product-compliance
Lightning Source LLC
La Vergne TN
LVHW020642100826
845148LV00012B/2293
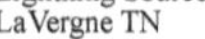

* 9 7 8 0 6 1 5 8 9 0 6 5 4 *